Trevor,

XMAS '92

Merry Christmas!

Robert
Jon
Holt

This is a delightful and fast-paced story for readers of all ages. It begins three days before Christmas.

Earl the Whirl---an expert at any game of chance with an edge---is an over-the-hill grifter. Though his hands are still quicker than the eye, he finds his mind beginning to slow.

The street-smart Deuce---a 12-year-old orphan---makes a living shining shoes on the streets of San Diego. At night, he often sleeps on a row of chairs pushed under a table at the San Diego City Library.

When Earl the Whirl and Deuce meet up, it becomes a contest of wits between two con artists.

Then Tanya Toogood---a spry lady who dresses like a teenager---skips into the picture. She presents Earl with a new challenge, and he soon becomes confused. Who is setting up whom?

Before the surprise ending, both Deuce and Earl the Whirl discover---through each other---the value of **honesty and giving**.

*Publisher's Note: We encourage you to read this story **out loud** with family and friends. It is divided into 3 parts. For your convenience, there are lists of characters for the chapters on pages 12, 84, and 122. Assign characters among your family and friends. Enjoy!*

Robert Lawrence Holt is the author of several other books. His works of fiction include:

Sweetwater: Gunslinger 201 ---a swashbuckling saga of aircraft carrier pilots.
Good Friday ---the oilfields of Saudi Arabia are threatened.
Peacemaker ---the U.S. launches the ultimate Star Wars weapon, that can think for itself.
Havana Hit ---Castro encounters forces beyond his control.

Non-Fiction:

The Complete Book of Bonds ---Harper & Row
Straight Teeth: Orthodontics ---William Morrow
How Mothers & Others Stay Slim ---Calif. Health Publications
How To Publish, Promote, & Sell Your Own Book ---St. Martin's Press

(for ordering information, see last page)

The Christmas Ruby

A novel by

ROBERT LAWRENCE HOLT

First Edition

Pacific Rim Press

Copyright © 1991 by Robert Lawrence Holt

All rights reserved. Reproduction or publication of the content in any manner, without express permission of the publisher, is prohibited. For information, address Reader Inquiry Branch, Editorial Department, Pacific Rim Press, P.O. Box 220, Carlsbad, CA 92018

(for ordering information, see last page)

Pacific Rim Press
Playa del Pacifica
P O Box 220
Carlsbad, CA 92018

Cover by Kelly Killough Studios
Encinitas, California

First Printing 1991

1 2 3 4 5 6 7 8 9

PRINTED IN THE UNITED STATES OF AMERICA

-----there is a Santa Claus. I know.
   For 52 years,
      my Mother has told me so!

                         ....RLH

Preface

The second most-frequently asked question of a new author is: *What made you write this book?* Initially, most books are dreams in the minds of their creators.

In the case of *The Christmas Ruby*, it actually was a dream. I awoke one morning---seven years ago---having had this extremely vivid dream. Two of the three persons appearing in it resem-bled real people.

As my dream began, a young boy (*Deuce* in the book) was shining shoes in front of a shoe store.

The owner of the shoe store (*Mr Weinstein* in book) had the appearance and manners of a gracious man who was an LA diamond merchant in my stockbroker days. He was a client, and I regret now that I cannot recall his name (that was 1965). This gentle, frail man would ride the Greyhound buses throughout Southern California---clusters of diamonds rolled up in handkerchiefs within the pockets of his suit---trading with jewelry store owners in small cities and towns. He was quite old and would rest in my downtown LA office while waiting for a bus to take him home to Beverly Hills.

Earl the Whirl (in my book) had to be inspired by George C. Scott in *The Flim-Flam Man.* It is one of my favorites. I saw the movie on television about a year prior to my dream. While the character in my dream did not resemble Scott physically or have his mannerisms, Earl was of the same age and had the same goal.

Back to the dream. It began with Deuce shining shoes on a sidewalk in front of Mr Weinstein's shoe store. The storeowner invites Deuce inside to help shelve boxes. He tests the honesty of the boy --- Deuce barely passes --- then leaves the store in the boy's hands for a few minutes to make a phone call down the block. My dream then followed what happens in the book up to the point where Deuce and Earl the Whirl meet. Then, I woke up.

After spending five years in the writing of *The Christmas Ruby*, it is the shortest of my ten books. I see this as an advantage. The holidays around Christmas are much too busy for a longer story. And the length of this book is just right for a Hollywood screenplay. Perhaps, I'll have one ready by the time the book's optioned.

I do hope you'll read this book with someone. Reading together can be a pure joy. I've done this with James Herriot, Edward Abbey, and a number of other fine authors. Currently, I'm enjoying Robert Grave's *I, Claudius* in this manner.

Three years ago, I founded the initial chapter of the Shakespearean Surfing Society ... for the purpose of reading out loud his comedies and those of other playwrights. We gather every few months to "act" out a comedy in one of our homes. The feast of food we have at mid-play is in the best Shakespeare tradition ... especially the chocolate pudding pie.

RLH

Acknowledgements

Normally...behind a successful author are several fine editors. In the writing of this book, I've had my share.

Ken Carter of Carlsbad, California, has edited it from the beginning ... through three title changes and three new first chapters. Ken is an excellent writer in his own stead, having won an award in the most recent International Raymond Chandler Imitation Writing Contest. Thanks for steering me in all the right directions, Ken.

Patricia Valiton, an editor in the Publications Office of the University of California/San Diego, provided invaluable advice and the fine tuning of a professional.

The well-known international linguist, Eileen Bach-y-Rita, lent a critical eye which led to many improvements. Catherine Yamada, a specialist in modern American literature, gave the manuscript a close reading. Mary Lane was quite helpful with the vernacular of the street.

Special mention is deserved by the Southern California artist, Kelly Killough, who took time from a busy schedule to compose and paint the striking watercolor which is the basis for the cover. He accurately captured the essence of each of the characters. Thanks for the midnight oil, Kelly.

I have benefited immensely by the support and forthright criticism of my loving parents for my books, including this one. And thank you, Barbara, for your attention to the words that follow ... and for holding both my hand and heart as *The Christmas Ruby* came to be.

RLH

Table of Contents

Preface
Acknowledgements

PART ONE - *Three Days to Christmas*

1	The Rattle of the Rolex	13
2	Tip the Show	22
3	A Parrot from Costa Rica	34
4	The Tenfold Return	39
5	For the Sake of a Bone	45
6	Tommy-Be-Good	54
7	Black Satin Pumps	61
8	The Condor	71
9	A Midnight Snack	78

PART TWO - *Two Days Till Christmas*

10	Serve The Hungry Hunter	85
11	The Game's Called Monte	91
12	Perfect Pear	102
13	An Honest Day's Work	109
14	One..Maybe Two	114

PART THREE - *The Day Before Christmas*

15	It Looks Like a Ruby	123
16	See You At Noon	130
17	Don't Like Being Jabbed	136
18	Thanks for Covering	142
19	A Piece of Mistletoe	149

❄ **Part One** ❄

Three Days Till Christmas

Characters & *Props* in Part One*

1. Earl the Whirl - *deck of cards, ring with jewel, watch, hat, toothpick, flightbag*
   Barracuda (cardplayer)
   Guppie "
   Dolphin "
   Octopus "
   Bus Driver

2. Cowpusher - *cowboy hat, neck chain*
   Mr Weinstein
   Spike, Cruz, Joe (3 punks)
   Thunderthighs - *with baby stroller & baby*

3. Old Lady - *2-wheeled cart, too-large robe, men's boots*
   Earl the Whirl - *chair, newspaper*

4. Deuce - *3 quarters, small book*
   Mr Weinstein

5. Deuce - *small book, shoe boxes, short stool, sandals*
   Mr Weinstein - *two glasses, large book*
   Maria
   1st Girl
   2nd Girl

6. Earl the Whirl

   1st Paramedic
   2nd Paramedic
   Deuce - *short stool, small wad of paper*
   Tommy-Be-Good - *shoe boxes, chair*
   Tommy's Mother - *chair*

7. Deuce - *play money*
   Earl the Whirl - *women's heels, 2 coins, ring box*
   Tanya Toogood - *big sunglasses, fez, rings*
   Trixie (her poodle) - *long rhinestone leash*

8. Earl the Whirl - *background music*
   Tanya Toogood
   Headwaiter - *2 chairs & table*

9. Earl the Whirl - *ring box w/ring*
   Tanya Toogood - *key*
   Trixie

* choose one person to read non-conversation and another to handle the props for each chapter.

1

The Rattle of the Rolex

It started out as a friendly game of blackjack.
   The older gent in the flat Panama hat had begun the deal when the Greyhound bus left Phoenix. His name was T. Earl Stengal --- though in certain circles he was better known as *Earl the Whirl.*
   While dealing the cards, he rolled an ivory toothpick back and forth across his lower lip. If one of the players made the mistake of looking at him too long, Earl would open his mouth in a wide, toothy grin and flip the toothpick end over end with his tongue. The habit discouraged staring.
   Most newcomers found it hard not to stare at Earl. His powder blue slacks and blue-and-cream checkered jacket were a bit garish, even for Southern California. And there was an odd orange glow to his deeply-tanned face...from a daily quart of carrot juice.

His left hand, which held the deck of cards, prominently displayed a gold ring crowned by a large red jewel.

On his other hand, the solid silver links of a loose watchband jangled with each throw of a card. The metallic sound was music to the ear of Earl the Whirl, who referred to it as *the rattle of the Rolex.*

The action in the back of the bus made the seven-hour ride to San Diego seem much shorter to the four other players. By design, since leaving Phoenix, the man in the Panama hat had lost an average of $10 to each of them.

As one of his players debated whether to take a hit, Earl glanced out the window ... and winced. On the point of a passing hill, his eyes had spotted a house brightly decorated with Christmas lights. The sight of it gave him a fleeting sense of loneliness.

A freeway sign flashed 'Alpine' and Earl checked his watch. The Greyhound was 30 minutes out of San Diego.

"Folks," began the con man, "how about something a little more exciting?"

Earl the Whirl glanced around at his school of fish.

The one he'd dubbed *Barracuda* grinned back. The sharp-toothed man had been begging for bigger bets all the way from Yuma.

Earl had purposely kept the maximum bet at a quarter though --- to keep his prey hungry.

On the other hand, *Guppie* frowned at the suggestion. The small-headed man made nothing but cautious bets with his cards, and it had not been easy for Earl to lose $10 to him.

Hearing the con man's proposal, *Dolphin* leaned back with a lazy smile. Earl had enjoyed the company of the pleasant, mild-mannered man and intended to see that Dolphin did better than the others.

Octopus was busy. His long fingers were rearranging his latest cards. Several times earlier, Earl had to ask the nervous man not to wrinkle the cards as he fruitlessly recounted his totals whenever they failed to please him.

"Tell you what," suggested Earl. "Let's finish this hand and play a simpler game."

Getting no objections, he finished out the hand of blackjack and gathered in the cards.

"All we do in this game," Earl explained, "is turn the two top cards face-up and take turns betting whether the next card will fall between them. An ace counts as a one."

It was a simple enough game ... and swift. In more than 50 years of gambling, Earl the Whirl had never found another card game that removed cash as quickly from the pockets of the greedy.

"Everybody put a buck in the pot," advised the con man, throwing four quarters onto the flat suitcase they used for a table.

Barracuda, Dolphin, and Octopus tossed in their antes. Guppie reluctantly followed suit.

"You win from the pot the amount of your bet," added Earl.

Placing the deck on the suitcase, Earl turned over the first two cards --- a *4 and a 10.*

Earl the Whirl pointed to Barracuda, the man on his left.

"You go first," said the con man. "Make a bet that the next card falls between those two."

Barracuda smirked. "This is like taking candy from a baby."

That's right, thought the con man, keeping a straight face. In a rite he performed for luck at the start of each con, Earl brought the ring on his left hand up to his chin and ran its smooth red stone along his skin.

Pulling a $5 bill from his wallet, Barracuda threw it on the suitcase. "I'll bet the whole pot!"

The sharp-toothed man grabbed the first card off the top of the deck and flipped it over. His eyes flared.

It was a queen.

Earl pointed to the next man in the circle.

"You're up," he told Dolphin.

The cheerful man dropped a $10 bill over the pot. "Guess I'll have to take your money, gentlemen."

He reached over to pick up the next card on the deck ... and the smile became pained as Dolphin set a 2 down.

Twenty bucks, mused the con man. A good start. Earl the Whirl enjoyed the thrill of the game, and he genuinely regretted he didn't get to play it more often. But it was not a game for friends, acquaintances or anyone else he was apt to run into a second time.

With a knitted brow, Octopus was leaning over to stare at the *4 and 10*.

Earl checked his watch and commented: "Hope this bus speeds up a bit. I've got to make a train connection to San Clemente."

Octopus swiveled his head to stare just as hard at the losing cards off to the side.

"Come on," complained Barracuda, who already had more cash in his fist for another bet.

Octopus reached over to lift the next card off the face-down deck.

Earl shot a hand out to stop him. "You have to bet first."

With a frustrated look, Octopus placed a $5 bill on the suitcase. He turned over the next card.

"Hah, a six!" beamed Octopus. "I win."

Giving Octopus $10 from the pot, the con man nodded with a pleased expression. The winner hadn't won all the pot. Earl the Whirl gathered the cards, reshuffled, and set the deck on the suitcase.

The first two cards he turned face-up this time were an *ace and a 9*.

Earl looked to Guppie. "Your turn."

With seven possible winning cards between the *ace and 9*, Earl knew the odds for success were slightly better than even. It was a good time to bet the pot. But not Guppie, thought Earl.

And Guppie proved him right. The careful man put only a dollar out for his bet...and promptly turned over a 5.

"You win, too," said Earl, pushing four quarters to Guppie.

Again shuffling the cards, Earl turned over a *7 and a queen.*

The con man welcomed the appearance of the queen. Players always bet more when a face-card turned up, even if the spread was less ... as it was this time. There were only four possible winning cards --- poor odds for any bet.

Might as well sweeten the pot anyway, decided Earl, and he put all of his $1 bills, six of them, atop the other cash on the suitcase. It wouldn't hurt to lose a little now, he figured.

Earl turned over a 7.

"Dang!" muttered the con man, shutting his eyes tight in pretended disappointment.

Again, Barracuda bet the pot, throwing a $20 bill onto the suitcase. With his other hand, he was already lifting the top card off the deck.

The face of the anxious man froze again. He flung down a 5 in disgust.

Dolphin was eyeballing the $40 pot.

And Earl eyeballed his fish, reading their thoughts. It looked so easy to win the inviting pile of green cash. All you had to do was put your money down and pick up the next card. A chance at fast cash made most men forget about figuring the odds.

Everyone watched Dolphin remove three tens from his wallet. With a carefree manner, Dolphin tossed his money on the growing pile.

He turned over a 3.

Dolphin merely shrugged at his bad luck.

Now, the pot was $70.

It always amazed Earl how the fish could never manage to lose fast enough at the game. As the cash stacked up, the sight of it would make the betting even wilder.

Whenever he felt a pang of conscience at winning their money, Earl would remind himself that it was not his fault. The fish were simply taking advantage of themselves.

Having won on his first try, Octopus hardly hesitated this time. He studied the *seven and queen* only a moment before placing a $50 bill on the suitcase. Giving the other players a confident grin, Octopus reached for his card.

At the sight of its flip-side, his face puckered as if he'd sucked a sour lemon. Octopus slowly brought the card to his nose.

"What is it?" demanded Barracuda, peering over the other man's shoulder.

"You've got a 6," stated the sharp-toothed man, and he turned to Guppie.

"Make your bet," urged Barracuda, eager to gamble again.

Guppie would not be rushed. His eyes kept going from the $120 cash pot to the face-up *7 and queen*. After he'd spent a half-minute calculating his chances, Guppie put $10 on the pot. His card came up a 9.

"This is easy!" exclaimed Guppie, scooping up $20 from the pot.

Earl gathered the cards, reshuffled, and turned two new cards over. A *4 and a king*.

In the next 10 minutes, the $110 pot topped out just over $400. Earl had won $100 with relatively small bets as the pot built.

The game's climax was as usual.

Barracuda, Dolphin, and Octopus suddenly found themselves running out of cash. And what little they had left was not enough to make a decent bet when a wide spread did appear. Guppie continued to wager modest amounts ... winning the same.

When Barracuda's turn came around, he pulled a watch off his wrist and held it up to Earl.

"This cost me $200 bucks!" declared Barracuda. "I want to bet it."

Earl the Whirl rolled the ivory toothpick to a corner of his mouth and let it pause, as if he were seriously considering the proposal. Earl had expected the request. Sooner or later, it usually came up. The con man eyed the watch, but he did not wish to win it from the fish. Accepting jewelry was risky business.

The last time Earl had taken jewelry was when he'd acquired his gold ring with the red stone. It was a big-stakes game, and the previous owner had claimed the gem was a ruby. It was not until later --- in sunlight --- that Earl saw the gem's color assume a greenish cast and knew he'd been fooled.

Pushing the brim of his white Panama higher on his forehead, Earl the Whirl shook his head no.

"I've got a better idea," offered the con man, giving his standard reply. "Since some of you are getting low on funds, why don't we let our bets pay off double?"

"Yeah!" agreed Barracuda. Octopus and Dolphin nodded quick agreement.

The cash began to disappear from the pot, and the fish barely noticed that Earl was winning most of it. The con man was careful not to win more than $40 to $50 at a time. And whenever he lost, Earl complained as loudly as anyone of his bad luck. Over the next 15 minutes, Earl removed $250 more from the pot.

Earl again glanced at his watch. Five minutes until the bus pulled into the station.

By beginning to deal planted cards off the cellar of his deck, Earl the Whirl arranged for the remaining money in the pot to be distributed between the three losers ... giving Dolphin the lion's share.

As the Greyhound pulled into the terminal, the last cash on the suitcase was won by Guppie.

Perfect timing, Earl told himself. It was important to conclude the game precisely when the bus ended its run. Too soon, and the fish would have time to discuss how badly they'd been hooked. Too late, and the con man might not make as easy an exit.

Checking his watch again, Earl grumbled: "This bus is 12 minutes late. I'm going to have trouble making my train connection."

Though the Greyhound had not come to a full stop, some of its passengers were getting out of their seats to recover luggage and Christmas packages in the overhead racks. Earl also stood and, grabbing his red TWA flightbag, started down the aisle. Over his shoulder, he called out:

"Thanks for the game, gentlemen."

The con man was at the front of the bus when Octopus finished his calculations. "I've lost over $100!" he growled.

Barracuda waved his thin wad of cash. "I dropped more than *twice* that!"

The two men looked to Dolphin, who calmly told them: "I've lost about $50 bucks."

Barracuda sprang out of his seat. "We've been swindled!"

"Yeah!" echoed Octopus.

"Let's catch up with that guy," suggested Barracuda, "and have a little talk with him."

They found it impossible to exit the bus quickly as the aisle was clogged with passengers. The two men were midway up the aisle as Earl the Whirl stepped onto a different bus only four gates away from the Phoenix Greyhound.

The driver of the other bus extended his hand to Earl for a ticket.

"How soon are you leaving?" asked Earl.

"Right now, mister."

"Copacetic," commented the con man.

"Huh?" questioned the driver.

Earl pressed a $10 bill into the driver's palm. "Can you let me off about five blocks from the station?"

The bus driver cocked an eye at the strange request.

"There's a lady I'm trying to avoid," explained the con man with a sly grin.

The driver took the money and motioned the man forward.

Five blocks later, Earl the Whirl stepped out onto the streets of San Diego. It was mid-evening, and he would have to find a cheap hotel.

San Diego was a favorite stop on his route. Yet, as Earl walked past the windows of stores gayly-decorated for the holidays, he sensed a sadness.

In three days, it would be Christmas --- not the best of times for a vagabond.

2

"Tip the Show"

The bare knees of the shoeshine boy ground into the sidewalk as the blazing sun seared the nape of his neck. Squinting through reflected light off the white concrete, he kept up the rhythm of the rag over the toe of the cowboy boot. The blinding glare seemed to magnify the heat ... or, thought the boy, the heat magnified the glare.

So far, the action was slow for a Monday morning. With Christmas shoppers too busy to stop and the businessmen scarce, most of his customers were like this one --- those who came downtown seeking casual recreation ... or selling the same. It didn't help that San Diego was in an unseasonable heat wave and had been for the last week.

Even more than the hot sun, the shoeshine boy felt the eyes of the customer boring down on him ... studying his strange features.

After the customers gawked at his odd appearance for a while, half of them would begin to ask questions. A few moments earlier, the boy had caught the fixed stare of the man, and now he wondered how long it would be before the first question.

The boy's eyes roamed above the boa cowboy boots and took in the tight, jade-colored slacks worn by the slim man. A long silver chain drooped over the man's Dire Straits tanktop, while a wide-brimmed Stetson shaded his eyes. From one ear, a dime-sized gold coin dangled. At the lobe of the other, a diamond caught the bright sunlight. Both coin and diamond flashed to and fro as the man's head bobbed to the cadence of the snapping rag.

Bearing down with a flourish, the 12-year-old boy pondered the status of his customer: pothead? ...cowboy? ...pusher? Glancing up again, he met the semi-glaze of the man's dilated eyes and took the last two.

A *cowpusher*, mused the boy, returning to the toe.

The choice wasn't encouraging. He knew pushers either gave a fat tip ... or, when they were too high to remember, none at all. The boy wondered if this was the one --- the dealer who'd sold Ruth the last drugs she'd ever take.

Something from behind snagged the foot of the shoeshine boy and yanked him off-balance. His shoulder slammed into the concrete. Still holding the rag taut in both hands, Deuce turned his head in the direction of malicious laughter.

"Don't take up the whole sidewalk, Short-stuff!" jeered his assailant.

Three boys --- a Latino, a black, and the white who had spoken --- continued down the sidewalk. Each sported a tall tuft of stiff hair down the center of his closely-trimmed scalp.

"Don't pay 'em no mind, kid," cautioned Cowpusher, sounding scared of the three bullies.

As Deuce returned to a kneeling position, he rubbed his bruised shoulder and scowled at the trio. Every few steps, one of the punks looked back to check if Deuce was coming after them. After massaging his shoulder a bit more, he returned to the boot.

Later, when Deuce's head began to reel, he instinctively raised up to straighten his knees and let the blood circulate again ... his hands still dancing high and slapping the wax-slickened rag over the pointed toe of the boot.

The rag made a smart sound, which did little for the toe ... but the boy knew his trade. The old shoeshine man in the U.S. Grant Hotel had once told him: "They tip the show, not the shine."

Shifting his weight from knee to knee to lessen the agony, the boy wished he hadn't forgotten the squares of thick leather which served as kneepads. The bus had come early, forcing him to rush out of the apartment and sprint two blocks before pulling himself onto the bike rack of the bus. A bead of sweat tickled his brow, and he paused to draw his forearm across it.

Cowpusher, unimpressed, grumbled in a Western drawl, "Ya best put on some mo' wax, kid ... 'fore ya wear out mah toe."

Time to go for it, the boy decided. It worked two times out of three, and a dandy like this one was even better odds. Dabbing a finger in his can of clear shoe wax, Deuce smeared it over the toe and looked up with a deadpan expression.

"Wanna spitshine, Mister?"

Cowpusher's bobbing head didn't stop as his dull eyes studied the torn collar of the boy's faded green shirt, polish-stained blue shorts, and beatup sneakers. The frayed shirt was stretched tight over the boy's chunky torso, and his thighs bulged from the too-small shorts. One rear pocket held a pint-sized amber bottle and the other a coverless paperback book. Not relishing the idea of the boy's spit on his three-hundred dollar boots, Cowpusher shook his head.

"Nah, jes polish 'em."

Continuing to rub in the wax, the boy pulled the amber bottle from his pocket and held it up. The label said: *Wild Turkey Blended Whiskey*. The man paused to peer at the bottle, then straightened with a sneer.

"Ya pushin' the wrong stuff, kid." The sneer slipped into a tight smile. "Ya lookin' to deal?"

"This isn't booze," declared the boy, holding the bottle higher. "It's *pure* distilled water ... for spitshining."

Examining the bottle again, Cowpusher asked: "How much extra?"

"Fifty cents."

"Go 'head, kid." The dangling coin and diamond resumed dancing to some inner rhythm.

Suppressing a grin, the boy popped a few drops of water from the bottle onto the toe of the boot and smacked his rag over it again. The amber bottle had been filled from the drinking fountain of the public library on Saturday. Within seconds, the toe glistened like a mirror.

"What's yore name?" inquired Cowpusher in a vague tone.

This was the first question most customers asked, if they were talkative. The boy preferred the quiet types.

"Deuce," he offered after a short silence. The name had been picked off a racing form by his mother.

Cowpusher pulled a pack of Marlboros from his hip and lit one. Expelling a cloud of smoke over the boy's head, he remarked: "I ain't nevah hearda nobody --- black or white --- with a tag like *thet*."

Maybe I'm not black or white, silently countered Deuce, hurrying to finish the first boot.

Cowpusher carelessly flicked his cigarette, and some of the ash landed on the boy's arm. Deuce winced and blew it off as the man continued to stare at his square face and broad pug nose.

"Where'd ya get them blue eyes ... and thet frizzy blond hair?"

If he tried to answer, Deuce knew it would only lead to more questions. He also knew an inquisitive customer tired quicker if there was no response, so the boy remained mute and applied more water to the toe.

Deuce thought to ask his own question: had Cowpusher known Ruth? She was gone. It had been three months now ... three months since he'd viewed her pale hands and face within the velvet-lined casket.

Actually, Ruth had been gone a long time before that. The last time she'd made a visit to the apartment was late one night in July. Whoever left her had rapped on the door and disappeared. When his aunt opened it, there his mother was --- huddled semi-conscious on the doormat, like a freezing dog.

A week later, she cleared out when the drugs cleared up. It had always been like that.

"Ya got a white mama, kid?"

Deuce barely nodded to confirm the partial truth.

Taking a long drag off his butt, Cowpusher spoke in a friendlier tone.

"Ya got nice colah ... same as my earring."

Ruth had been half-white and half-black, which explained the boy's blue eyes and even the tightly-curled hair, but the deep golden skin had come from someplace else. When Deuce was five and starting school, he'd inquired about his father.

His mother, closing her eyes in a dreamy smile, had told him:

"Your daddy was the grandest man *I ever* saw. Way over six feet, with muscles of a giant. He was Samoan ... and gold as the sun!"

She'd been with him but once and forgotten the name. Deuce's mother had made a joke of it ... telling her only child she hadn't known her own father either.

Flicking his butt into the gutter, Cowpusher asked: "Whatcha do with the money ya make buffing shoes?"

With more force than necessary, Deuce beat a heat over the toe.

He normally recited his "going to college" story. It worked well with businessmen --- who tipped more if it was "savings" for college. But street people needed another story. Their money would go for clothes, usually something in a style worn by the customer.

Deuce debated between the boa boots and Stetson. Or even to say it would be spent on Christmas presents.

A weak rasp of a cough caused the boy to glance over his shoulder in its direction. Deuce recognized the fragile, bone-white face of Mr Weinstein --- the elderly owner of the shoe store before which he'd been snaring customers the past week. The well-dressed storeowner wore the same grey, three-piece suit he'd worn on the other days.

On the previous day, when neither of them had customers, Mr Weinstein had come out of his store to chat. Deuce had tolerated the intrusion. The frail body of the shoe store owner was the same height as the five-foot-five boy... and more important, Mr Weinstein didn't ask the questions.

He didn't seem to care why a dusky-skinned boy with an Oriental slant to his eyelids had blue eyes and curly blond hair.

Deuce tapped the cowboy boot of his customer, indicating it should be taken off the shoebox and replaced by the other one.

Mr Weinstein turned away and slowly cranked a long metal rod, drawing out an awning that shaded his storefront. With the awning in place, he leaned against the doorway and dabbed at a watery eye with his handkerchief. While the storeowner spoke in an Old World accent and dressed like a preacher, Deuce almost liked him. He hadn't told the boy to move on like other storeowners.

A woman's screech tore the air.

At a bus stop down the block, Deuce spotted the white punk who'd tripped him. The youth was in a tug-of-war over a purse with a heavy-thighed redhead wearing terry-cloth shorts and halter. The Latino and black youths stood posed with raised fists, facing off the other people at the bus stop. A squealing two-year-old in a stroller beside the shrieking redhead added its own protests to the clamor.

"Will ya look at thet?" marveled Cowpusher. "The All-American T-team meets *Thunderthighs!*"

Built like a Viking warrior goddess and outweighing her opponent by an easy hundred pounds, the woman started to swing both purse and punk in a wide arc.

On the first revolution, the white youth stumbled over the stroller. Still holding onto the purse's strap, he too began hollering for help. Thunderthighs was now swinging him completely off his feet and proceeded to bowl over his partners as well.

The Latino, recovering his feet, grabbed the white punk's legs on the next revolution, causing the strap of the purse to break. Both youths fell to the sidewalk with the woman, but she held only the strap of her purse now. Her indignant screeches came even louder as the three thieves ran wildly down the sidewalk. They came in the direction of the shoe store ... the white tough leading with the purse.

Cowpusher flattened himself against the window of the store. Gripping the handle of his shoebox, Deuce crouched beside his customer. Mr Weinstein retreated within his doorway.

As the thieves came by, Deuce swung his box around.

It caught the white punk square in the gut, folding his body in a ball. The purse kept going, the two other thieves sprawling over the first one.

Diving for the purse, Deuce grabbed it just as a dark hand reached over to do the same.

"Come on, Short-stuff!" barked the black youth. "Leggo!"

The black, a sturdy six-footer, jerked on the purse but it was no contest.

Gripping the purse with burly hands, Deuce easily pulled it to his body. The contest evened when a hard object clipped him in the jaw. Stunned, Deuce looked in the direction of the blow in time to see the Latino's foot coming again. Clinching his eyes tight, Deuce sensed a thud but felt no pain.

Deuce thought he was unconscious, but something was wrong. He could still see. Clearly. He stared up into the Latino's startled face as the punk's eyes rolled and his body collapsed in a heap.

Seeing the black youth devoting his attention elsewhere, Deuce wrenched the purse free and rolled away.

The black youth, on hands and knees, was watching the long metal rod that wavered in the hands of Mr Weinstein. Whether the old man could raise the rod high enough to deliver a second blow was beginning to look doubtful when the noise level in the vicinity increased.

High-pitched shrieks and the clopping of clog heels announced the arrival of Thunderthighs. Her fire-red hair was flared out like a cat in fright.

"*Gimme my bag!*" shrilled the horn-mad woman. "*Gimme my bag!*"

Her puffed hair-style seesawed side to side as she shoved the stroller before her. The howls of the baby nearly drowned out the bellowing of its mother.

Clutching his mid-section, the white thief staggered from the gutter and muttered: "Let's get outta here, Joe."

"What 'bout Cruz?" the black youth snapped.

The white youth shoved a toe into the ribs of the groaning Latino, who barely stirred.

"Leave 'im!" snarled the white youth.

Joe bent over Cruz and grabbed his arm, bringing the Latino to his knees. Looking to the white punk, Joe shouted: "Come on, Spike ... help me!"

The Viking steamroller roared up as Joe and Spike dragged Cruz away.

"We'll be back, Short-stuff!" shouted Spike over his shoulder.

Deuce was still on his knees when Thunderthighs rushed upon him.

"Gimme my bag!" she angrily repeated.

When Deuce offered the purse, the woman --- failing to distinguish him from the three thieves --- snatched it away. Without another word, she did a wheelie with the stroller and was on her way.

Feeling at his tender jaw, Deuce watched Thunderthighs pound away. He, the old man, and Cowpusher were astounded at the sight. Each of the woman's huge and perfectly-rounded buns was doing a double-hop to the staccato of her clog heels. But this was not what astonished them.

In the tug-of-war, one side of the woman's terry-cloth shorts had ridden halfway up. The bared bun displayed a tattoo of a multi-colored butterfly ... in full flight.

"Lady!" called out Mr Weinstein. "This boy *saved* your purse!"

The giant butterfly continued fluttering down the sidewalk to the noisy tempo of the clog heels. When Thunderthighs disappeared around the corner, Cowpusher broke the silence.

"Here, kid." He held out a dollar to Deuce.

The boy still watched the corner, as if hoping the woman would reappear. Mr Weinstein came forward and demanded of the pusher.

"Why did you not help us?"

The gold earring jerked as Cowpusher placed both hands on his hips in a prissy pose.

"You *crazy*?" sputtered Cowpusher. "They mighta had knives!"

Getting stared down by the aged man, Cowpusher twisted back to Deuce and offered the dollar again. "Hey, ya want the money?"

Unhearing, the preoccupied boy lowered his eyes in resignation. The woman, whose hair had resembled that of his mother, would not return. He bent to the task of recovering the contents of his shoebox, picking up a spring-grip hand exerciser first.

"Yore crazy, too!" exclaimed Cowpusher, jamming the dollar back in his pocket. The boa boots stomped off in the same direction as the clog heels.

As Deuce examined his shoebox, he spoke in an undertone. "Thanks for backing me, old man."

The boy looked up. He couldn't tell whether the expression below Mr Weinstein's glassy eyes was a grimace or a smile. The storeowner was hunched forward --- clutching the metal rod for support --- and his feet were spread, as if he was having difficulty balancing.

"Please," he uttered in an infirm tone, "give me a hand."

The boy came up and stood awkwardly as Mr Weinstein transferred one hand to Deuce's shoulder and asked:

"Can you carry the rod?"

Taking the narrow pole, Deuce was surprised how heavily Mr Weinstein's hand rested on his shoulder. The boy took short steps to keep pace with the elderly man's shuffle. Once inside the store, Mr Weinstein indicated the nearest chair with a feeble wave. At the chair, he grasped its back and sank his body into it.

Seeing the storeowner's ashen face, Deuce asked:

"You alright?"

The reply was barely audible. "In the back ... on a wash basin. A bottle of white pills."

Deuce ran down a double row of back-to-back chairs, around the cash register counter, and pushed through a beaded curtain. The only light entering the windowless storeroom came through the curtain, and he hesitated, permitting his eyes to become accustomed to the darkness. A narrow cot gradually revealed itself beside a waist-high refrigerator. Lining the walls were oddly-spaced shelves crammed with shoeboxes and books. There appeared to be more books than shoes. Deuce cautiously entered and found the white bottle in a small bathroom built into a corner.

With trembling hands, Mr Weinstein removed two pills from the bottle and placed them under his tongue before leaning back.

"You need water?" Deuce asked uncertainly.

Shaking his head but once, Mr Weinstein pointed the boy to a chair beside him and closed his eyes.

Not having ventured into the store before, Deuce surveyed his surroundings. The double row of chairs evenly divided the 35-foot length of the store. Shelves of boxed shoes reached to the ceiling, and Deuce wondered how the storeowner reached the upper levels ... until he spotted sliding ladders attached to the top rows.

A countertop along the rear wall held an ancient cash register trimmed in bronze, plus wire display stands of wax, stockings, and shoe strings. On the wall behind the counter was a clock framed within an old Coca Cola sign. At the center of the wall was a Norman Rockwell print showing the man of the house napping in his easy chair as a cocker spaniel chewed on his fancy slippers. A few smaller picture frames held quotes too small to read from the front of the store.

Deuce began counting the boxes on the nearest wall.

3

A Parrot From Costa Rica

    T. Earl Stengal held an open newspaper just below his line of vision. The Panama hat atop his head tracked the likelier prospects in the lobby of the Hudson House like a periscope above water.
    A few sterile rows of dusty fluorescent tubes, some flickering in their last throes, gave off a light barely adequate for reading in the lobby.
    Without meaning to, Earl made eye contact with an old crone wearing a light orange bathrobe over her house dress. The robe matched her hair. She scuffed along in men's workboots that were too large, dragging a two-wheeled cart of groceries.
    Giving Earl a wide smile, the woman detoured toward him with the cart. He raised his newspaper higher.
    The thick odor of talcum powder announced her presence.
    "New here, ain't cha?" she prattled in a chummy voice.
    "Go away," Earl silently mouthed through his paper.

The orange-robed woman stepped to his side in order to view his face again.

"You dye your hair?" Her pointed chin nodded with the question, as if to confirm her suspicion.

You've got it backwards, mused Earl, looking the other way.

She raised a bent finger and pointed to the top of his head.

"Tain't your hair anyway, is it?"

Bringing his face around, Earl fixed the woman with a livid frown. If she could detect that in the poor light, he decided it was time to tint his eyebrows and mustache again, to match the dark-brown hairpiece.

The dim lobby of the Hudson House --- a pensioner's haven in a low-rent section of downtown --- was devoid of the grandeur it had known 90 years earlier when it'd been one of the premier hotels of San Diego. Its imported crystal chandeliers had been auctioned off in the 1930s when the first of six coats of mint-green paint had been applied to the bird's-eye maple paneling of the lobby. The only bright spot in its interior was a silver-foil Christmas tree, from which a few red ornaments hung.

"Ya don't look a day over 55," commented the crone in a friendlier tone, intent on entertaining herself a bit longer.

Though appreciative of the compliment, Earl pretended to concentrate on the newspaper. His hairpiece, porcelain caps on his teeth, and trim figure encouraged the general illusion that he was under 60. When asked, Earl claimed 54. He was 68.

The woman stepped nearer to study him.

"You wearing contacts, sonny?"

Earl shifted his newspaper to block her view. His own was aided by soft lenses, which he wore when on the prowl.

"I tried contacts once," said the woman. "They stung my eyes."

Earl glanced around for assistance. Directly across the lobby, behind an ornately-carved counter, was a student/clerk concentrating on his textbook under a low brass lamp. The only other people in the lobby were near its street entrance where a wooden telephone booth was built into a wall. It was one of the last public phones in downtown San Diego where a person could sit while talking. Before it, a short line of hotel patrons waited to make their calls.

To discourage loitering, the lobby contained one other place to sit --- the oaken straight-backed armchair occupied by Earl. It was upholstered in cracked but still intact leather.

"Where'd you migrate from?" cackled the crone, standing off a bit. "You look like a parrot from Costa Rica."

Taken aback, Earl's head dipped to examine his plumage. The blue-and-cream checkered sports coat was complemented by a lavender silk shirt open at the neck and the same powder-blue slacks he'd worn on the bus. Cream-colored stockings set off his white shoes.

"What time is it, peacock?" posed the woman. "I gotta be going."

Relieved at her impending departure, Earl promptly extended his counterfeit Rolex at arm's length to read it. At high noon each day, it was necessary to correct the watch's 21-minute error --- an act that caused Earl some resentment. Not at the timepiece's defectiveness, but from a sense that his customary morning leisure was being cut short.

He now added 19 minutes to what he saw. "Thirty-seven minutes after ten."

"*So, you can talk after all!*" twitted the woman in exaggerated satisfaction.

Earl peeked over his paper with admiration. He respected anyone who could outwit him. When his head disappeared again, she reached out.

His left hand recoiled at her touch, crinkling the newspaper.

"That's a queer wedding ring," she said, straight to his face. "Are ya married?"

In the artificial light, the raspberry-red jewel displayed on his ringfinger resembled a ruby, which is what Earl let people believe it was. Earl wore it prominently for the same reason he displayed the imitation Rolex --- to keep up appearances. In addition to believing himself to be a professional gambler, he fancied himself a lady's man.

The pencil-thin mustache on his spare yet handsome face --- plus the savoir-faire with which he executed his two favorite cons --- had prompted fellow members of his ignoble fraternity to dub him *Earl the Whirl*.

By way of answering the pesky woman, he shook his head then raised the newspaper again.

The two cons permitted him to pursue his quest. The first con (card and shell games with men) was worked when he was broke. The second con (with the ladies) built the money from the first con into a stake adequate for Atlantic City, Las Vegas, or anywhere else he could find a big-money game.

And his quest ... it was a quarter-million.

That would be enough, Earl always told himself, to finally retire from the vagabond life. That would be enough to set himself up in a business somewhere.

It was all a sham.

Once, Earl had even proved it to himself. A run of luck at roulette in Reno had given him a stack of chips worth $252,000. He could have walked, but suddenly, his goal changed to a third of a million. And if he could make that, why not a half-million?

Earl made the one-third million, and more.

Before the casino's luck improved, he topped out at $388,000. Twenty minutes later, instead of a half-million, Earl the Whirl walked out of the casino broke.

Not unhappy. Just broke. He had *a million-dollar story* to tell his fellow conmen.

And he could always start over. He knew that for certain. T. Earl Stengal had been starting over all his life.

4

"The Tenfold Return"

After losing count of the shoeboxes along the wall --- they tended to fade into each other --- for the third time, Deuce switched his attention back to Mr Weinstein.

The storeowner's rheumy blue eyes were now open. In a corner of one, a large tear had formed, and he dabbed at it with his handkerchief.

Deuce, embarrassed for the man, started to look away but caught an apologetic smile beginning on Mr Weinstein's face.

"I am not crying," said the aged man. "They are tears of my years."

It made little sense to the boy, who nodded toward the rear of the store.

"You live back there ... alone?"

"Yes." Mr Weinstein's smile widened. "And no."

Deuce wrinkled his brow in confusion. He was annoyed at the nervousness that forced his conversation.

"*Yes* to your first question," said the storeowner, "and *no* to the second one."

He must have a cat back there, thought Deuce. A dog would have barked at me.

"I live with my books," explained Mr Weinstein.

Now Deuce understood --- more fully than the storeowner could know. At school, the few Samoans shunned him for being a half-caste. The blacks called him "Oreo." And the Latinos and whites ignored him. Not fitting in their worlds, the boy had created his own.

He found it downtown. Deuce spent most evenings at Eighth and E Street --- the cavernous city library. Without a parent to help obtain a library card, Deuce did his reading at the tables beside the books. He waded through Stevenson, London, Mead, Michener, and other authors who wrote of the South Seas and his heritage.

The three-story building was *his* favorite home --- often the only one. When no other place was available, he slept there. To hide from the security guards at lights out, he would stretch out along the seats of chairs under a table.

During the day in poor weather, Deuce found shelter at the Iron Man Gym on 4th Avenue. He traded sweeping and hanging up the weights for the use of the facility. A few of the regulars called him "Iron Boy" in recognition of the unusual strength he'd developed in his hands and arms for a male his size.

Though Mr Weinstein dabbed at his eye, it continued to water.

The tears reminded Deuce of his mother. Years earlier, when they'd lived together --- between the deep depressions following the drugs --- she was full of laughter. Ruth had been more of a sister or playmate to her son than a parent. The two addressed each other by first names.

When told of his mother's final overdose, Deuce hadn't cried. Neither had his aunt, who said it was a merciful end to the self-torment. Later, in the night when the boy was alone, the tears had come. In the remembering.

Ruth had surprised her son the Christmas before with a second-hand bike. And Christmas Eve had been special, too. A few neighbors were invited over to sing carols. The bike was stolen a month later.

Deuce stood abruptly and announced: "I gotta find some customers."

Picking up his shoebox, he made for the door.

"Wait!"

The boy twisted around, his impatience showing.

"Maybe" ---the storeowner held his hands out--- "you could help with my customers."

Deuce didn't alter his pained expression. He had never worked for anyone before and wasn't sure he wanted to.

"What would you earn polishing shoes this afternoon?" Mr Weinstein asked.

Deuce started to say ten and thought better. "Fifteen dollars."

The beginning of a grin appeared on the storeowner's face as he nodded agreement and reached into a pocket. Extracting a money-clip and removing three tens, he offered the money to the boy.

"I require all my employees to wear white shirts and brown slacks."

Self-consciously tucking his tattered shirt into his stained shorts, Deuce muttered: "I got money."

Mr Weinstein extended his hand further. "I always loan the cost of these clothes to my employees. You can work it off."

"I don't need it." Deuce ended the discussion by pivoting and starting out the door.

A vision of the boy shoplifting crossed the storekeeper's mind and he called out: "Where will you get clothes?"

Deuce replied over his shoulder: "Goodwill."

When Deuce returned 30 minutes later, dressed as directed, Mr Weinstein came around the counter and studied the boy's soiled sneakers.

"Those don't match your slacks."

Getting no protest, he proceeded to fit Deuce with a pair of dark brown dress shoes.

When customers arrived, Mr Weinstein told Deuce which boxes to bring off the shelves; and between customers, he showed the boy how to restock from the backroom. The second time Deuce closely observed the storeowner pocketing the paper money after a purchase, Mr Weinstein pointed to the cash register.

"Do you wonder why I do not put the money in there?"

Deuce shrugged, pretending disinterest.

"How many times," Mr Weinstein posed, "do you think my store was robbed in the last year?"

The boy's shoulders rose and fell again.

"Three times," said Mr Weinstein softly.

Deuce pondered how the storeowner could make a living, getting robbed so often? Why did he even keep the store open?

Mr Weinstein read the cynical eyes.

"They ask for the money from there" ---he pointed a finger at the cash register--- "but never from me."

The boy dropped his eyes, feeling foolish for misjudging the man.

Mr Weinstein continued. "The register has only a ten, a five, and some ones---enough to make change." He paused. "That's all they get."

That's all they need, the boy calculated, for a dime of crack. They leave happy ... and most of the money stays here. The old pro's got it wired, thought Deuce, deciding to pay closer attention to him.

After the exit of a cranky woman who'd tried on several shoes without buying anything, Deuce noticed three quarters under the chair where she'd sat. The chair was close to the front door. Deuce shot a quick glance at Mr Weinstein who stood near the cash register at the other end of the store. The elderly man looked up at the same time and called out:

"Why don't we decorate the windows?"

Deuce followed him behind the beaded curtain where Mr Weinstein located several shoeboxes of Christmas decorations. They placed tinsel, colored bulbs, and greenery in the display windows on both sides of the front door. Across one window, they taped the letters, *Merry Christmas!*

When Mr Weinstein went behind the curtain again to get more tape, Deuce quickly scooped up the three quarters.

After taping another string of letters saying *Feliz Navidad!* to the other window, Deuce asked what the words meant.

"They mean 'Happy Nativity' answered the storeowner, "which is the traditional Christmas greeting in Mexico." After a pause, he added: "Though I'm not a Christian, I still enjoy the holidays. They're a good reminder to practice 'The Tenfold Return.'"

"What's that?" asked Deuce.

"It's on the wall." Mr Weinstein pointed behind the counter to a quote enclosed in a small gold frame.

"Whatever is given freely," recited the elderly man, "comes back tenfold."

Deuce thought it over and started to ask another question when a customer walked in. After selling a pair of shoes, Mr Weinstein suggested to Deuce that they take a break and asked: "Would you like some hot tea?"

The boy hesitated with a slightly bleak expression.

"I have apple juice, too," offered Mr Weinstein, heading toward the back. Sitting in a chair, the boy stared at the wall of boxes again, then remembered the discarded paperback he'd picked up at the library and pulled it off his hip. As was his habit, he also took the spring-grip exerciser from his shoebox and squeezed it as he read.

5

For the Sake of a Bone

After handing Deuce a glass of juice, Mr Weinstein blew at his tea and sat down beside the boy. "What do you read?"

"Just something I found," replied Deuce. He closed the book, uncertain how to pronounce its title.

The storekeeper leaned over to read the cover and nodded in approval. "So, you read Victor Hugo. Do you like the story?"

"It's okay," admitted the boy. Since taking the book from the library discard box two days earlier, Deuce had found it difficult to put down. He was halfway through it.

After a cautious sip at his steaming tea, the storeowner came to his feet again. Going into the backroom, he returned with a book and placed it in the boy's lap.

"Here is a gift," began Mr Weinstein, "for the holidays."

The leather binding of the book had faded, but the gold lettering embossed on its spine was still clear and bright. Deuce recognized the two words he'd been unable to pronounce on the cover of his paperback --- *Les Miserables.*

"It is a second edition, printed in 1863," explained Mr Weinstein. "Long before you, or even I, were born."

The boy wondered how he would grip the bike rack of the bus if he took the book. It was hard enough already with his shoe kit.

"Do you know who Napoleon was?" asked Mr Weinstein.

Deuce nodded.

"Victor Hugo," continued the storeowner, "was born the son of one of Napoleon's generals ... almost 200 years ago."

Flipping through the pages of the book, Deuce paused at an illustration.

"That's the prison where the main character suffered terribly," said Mr Weinstein.

Deuce studied the dismal, high-walled fortress on the page. Rows of small open windows lined the stone wall like pockmarks. It reminded him of the needle-tracks on his mother's legs and arms.

"I have no place to keep this book," said Deuce.

"Surely---" began Mr Weinstein.

"I live with my aunt," interrupted Deuce, looking away. "She moves a lot."

The storeowner spread his hands expansively. "Keep it in your room ... under your bed."

What room? Deuce reflected. What bed? When he could stay with his aunt, a worn-out sofa in the short hall off the kitchen served as his bed ... and the cockroaches ate what was left on the floor ... including paper.

"My aunt has lotsa guests," said the boy, hoping Mr Weinstein would get his point.

"So," smiled the storeowner indifferently, "maybe they would like to read the book also?"

Deuce knitted his brow. It wasn't working, but then few people did understand. "My aunt moves a lot," he repeated, "because she has problems with the law."

Mr Weinstein cocked his head at the boy.

Actually, Deuce told himself, I'm the one who moves a lot --- whenever she gets arrested and held over at rent-time. When he could, the boy attended his aunt's court appearances so he'd know when she'd be released again. Once a judge had suspended the sentence, calling the offense a *victimless* crime. Deuce had mulled over the word for several days. Did the hunger that gnawed in his stomach when the sentences weren't suspended make *him* a victim?

The answer to the question hadn't mattered for the last year --- not since he'd built the shoeshine kit at school. When need be, it fed him; and he actually welcomed the moves now. The neighbors and kids were friendly for a while at a new place ... until they came to know his aunt.

Deuce stared at the book with a glum expression. The stony silence within the store was broken by the sounds of passing cars.

Mr Weinstein, finally sensing the boy's meaning, changed the subject.

"Why did you swing your box at the thief?"

The boy swirled the ice in his glass, thinking over the question.

"Weren't you afraid?"

Deuce shook his head. He hadn't been, and now he wondered why not.

"Have you read Jack London?" asked the storeowner.

"Yes."

Mr Weinstein went on. "London once described youths who travel in wolf packs as cowards. They avoid fights unless they outnumber their victim."

Maybe I reacted, thought Deuce, because the woman's hair reminded me of my own mother. Or was it simply the wide-open gut of the unsuspecting punk? Too many times, he'd silently taken abuse from a swaggering tough who'd taunted him from the safety of a gang.

"I dunno why I swung my box," Deuce finally replied.

It was quiet in the shoestore for a minute.

Mr Weinstein took a deep breath, then spoke, drawing each word out with great care.

"*An honest person does not make himself a dog ... for the sake of a bone.*"

Deuce briefly locked eyes with Mr Weinstein, who looked at him with uncommon sternness.

The boy could not understand the relationship between the "honest person" statement and the three thieves ... until he realized none had been meant.

So the storeowner had seen the coins, decided Deuce. But the lady was gone, and it was too late to return the quarters to her. Finders-keepers, Deuce told himself.

Mr Weinstein stood and went to the store entrance, where he stopped, keeping his back to the boy.

Deuce pictured the coins falling to the carpet from the woman's dress or purse ... and winced as he saw *the bone*. The storeowner would surely have pointed out the coins to the woman. He had sat on a stool before her the entire time ... as Deuce brought shoeboxes from the shelves.

Realizing Mr Weinstein had planted the coins under the chair, Deuce got up and walked to the door where he held up his glass and asked: "Can I have some more juice?"

Mr Weinstein solemnly took the glass and headed toward the back. When he was behind the curtain, Deuce pulled the quarters from his pocket and rushed to the area where he'd found them. Which chair was it? he speculated.

Seeing Mr Weinstein coming through the beaded curtain, he awkwardly pitched the quarters under the nearest chair.

"I'm out of juice," announced Mr Weinstein, "so I'm bringing you water."

Deuce didn't move from his spot, trying to decide whether to screen the coins from the man's view or simply walk away from them.

Mr Weinstein stopped before the boy. He eyed the quarters a moment and spoke with a weary smile.

"You've dropped your money."

Deuce gaped at the three quarters, uncertain what to do or say.

Mr Weinstein felt sorry for the humbled boy. At the same time, he was immensely pleased Deuce had chosen to return the coins.

"They're not mine," said Deuce.

The storeowner stooped to pick up the coins and offered them to the boy. "Buy yourself a soda at the corner drug store."

"I---" Deuce started to protest.

Mr Weinstein dropped them in the pocket of the boy's shirt. "When I'm busy with a customer, why don't you help others who come in?"

Within 20 minutes, Deuce had sold his first pair of shoes and required only moderate help re-shelving. Shortly thereafter, he was refusing to divulge his name to three young Latino girls who had asked to be shown a variety of sandals. After building a large mound of rejected boxes, the boy excused himself to check with the storeowner.

"What should I do?" Deuce pleaded. "They keep asking for more and more."

"Be nice to them." replied Mr Weinstein, who had been watching in amusement from his tall chair behind the counter. "It looks good from the sidewalk to have customers inside."

The youngest girl --- called Maria by the other two --- hadn't asked to see anything; though, at the request of her friends, Deuce had brought most of the sandals for her. Except for a shy smile whenever Deuce met her eyes and an occasional giggle with the other girls, Maria had said little. But to the boy, her smile and eyes said everything. Each time their eyes met, Deuce felt a warm rush across his face.

He returned to the girls and stood before Maria, gazing at the violet shadow boldly painted over each of her downcast eyes. Red lipstick richly applied to her lips accented the rouge blush of her cheeks. Glossy black hair flowed over the girl's shoulders and down to her waist. When Maria raised her eyes, Deuce asked:

"Would you like to see the latest in dancing shoes?"

A quick smile flashed on Maria's face as she shot sideways glances to her companions. Deuce answered for them.

"I'll bring some."

Pulling an armload of boxes off the shelves, he also picked up the short stool upon which Mr Weinstein sat while fitting shoes. Before, the boy had let the girls fit their sandals by themselves. Sitting on the stool before Maria, Deuce made an elaborate show of removing a pair of bright red heels from their box.

"Your foot, please," he softly asked.

Maria's quieted companions watched as Deuce gingerly held the heel of her bare foot in his palm, then eased her toes into the red leather.

After a short silence, he observed in a satisfied voice. "Looks perfect."

"I want to see that in *my size!*" blurted out the oldest and prettiest of the trio.

Deuce studied the other girl's feet. Shrugging with a smirky smile, he told her:

"We don't carry them in a size large enough for you."

Deuce quickly switched his attention back to Maria: "Let's see how the other heel feels."

She beamed as he fitted the other shoe. Offering his hand to Maria in the manner he'd seen Mr Weinstein use with women customers, the boy repeated the storeowner's words.

"Would you like to stroll about in them?"

Taking his hand and keeping her eyes on the heels, Maria balanced herself awkwardly.

"There's a mirror over there," said Deuce, still holding her hand. As he led her the short distance, Maria struggled to keep her feet from twisting sideways. At the mirror, she released his hand and stood stiffly, admiring the heels and the new line they gave to her legs. Maria loudly whispered to her companions:

"They're terrific."

The other girls responded with sour expressions. Mr Weinstein, who'd busied himself nearby, broke the silence.

"Deuce, why don't you ask the young lady if she'd like us to put the shoes on hold for her?"

"Come on, Maria!" chirped the oldest girl, heading for the door. "We're going to be late for the movie."

Leading Maria to her chair, Deuce unhurriedly removed the heels and placed her sandals back on. When he finished and looked up, her eyes were waiting.

Gazing into her pretty black eyes, Deuce searched his mind, wishing to prolong the moment.

Maria waited for him to speak first, but he had no idea how to begin. He was eager to know where she lived and where she went to school. But it was the first time he'd wished to ask such questions of a girl, and he couldn't bring himself to say a word.

"Maria!" called out the oldest girl again.

The boy's smile faded as Maria flew out the door. He stood rooted where the girl had left him, suffering in his shyness.

"I'll help you shelve," offered the storeowner.

They worked silently until Deuce posed a question that had been on his mind.

"Mister, why are you keeping this store?"

The storeowner was stepping onto a ladder. He paused thoughtfully.

"To keep one of my three most-valued possessions." Mr Weinstein then proceeded up the ladder.

"What's that?" the boy inquired when the storeowner reached the top of the ladder.

"My health," replied the storekeeper.

"You work to keep your *health*?" scoffed the boy.

Mr Weinstein looked down with a patient nod.

"What're the other two possessions?" asked Deuce curiously.

"My education..." the storeowner drew out, "and my name."

A short pause.

"Those aren't possessions," countered Deuce, though he wasn't altogether sure what they were.

"But they are," nodded Mr Weinstein, starting down the ladder. At the floor, he softly added: "Easy to obtain ... but hard to keep."

Deuce squinted at the comment, but the words began to register.

Mr Weinstein continued. "No one can take them from you but yourself."

Thinking of his mother, Deuce remembered that he'd never seen anyone force her to take the pills and dope.

When all the sandals had been shelved, the storeowner went behind the counter and opened the register. After picking out a few coins, he said matter-of-factly:

"Will you take care of the customers until I get back?"

Deuce looked surprised.

"I must go to the drug store on the corner to make a phone call," explained Mr Weinstein.

He pointed to the cash register. "To open this, hit the double-O on the bottom row."

The old man closed the register drawer and, at an unhurried pace, walked out of his store.

6

Tommy-Be-Good!

The orange-robed crone---having covered every aspect of Earl the Whirl's appearance that she considered worthy of comment---had promised a return match with the con man and retired to her room in the Hudson House.

Earl then eased himself lower in the oak armchair and took a catnap in the quieted lobby.

When he awoke, a small crowd had gathered just within the entrance of the Hudson House. Neatly folding his paper, Earl got up to investigate. As he approached the commotion, he saw that a man had collapsed inside the wooden phone booth.

Placing his hands on the shoulders of those in front of him, Earl the Whirl repeated:

"Excuse me, I'm a physician."

His words melting a path to the booth, Earl knelt beside the grey-suited body. The man's breathing appeared normal to Earl, who suddenly pivoted on his knee and exclaimed to those nearest:

"*Move back! Give the man air.*"

Leaning over the chest of the unconscious man, Earl lowered his head to listen for a heartbeat. When the con man straightened, he again spoke with authority: "We've got to call an ambulance!"

With that, he abruptly stood and marched to the hotel desk. The student/clerk was still engrossed in his book.

"Young man," Earl formally began, "a gentleman at the phone booth---"

"Yeah, I know," interrupted the clerk, not bothering to look up. "Happens all the time around here. I've already called the paramedics."

After a thoughtful pause, Earl replied in a sarcastic tone.

"Copacetic."

"Huh?" The clerk looked up with a squint. "What'd you say?"

Earl the Whirl gave the uncaring clerk a look suggesting it would be beneath his dignity to repeat or explain himself.

Returning to the unconscious man, Earl heard the screeching of tires at the lobby entrance.

Two paramedics raced inside, the first carrying a folded stretcher and the second a medical case. Hastily checking the unconscious man, the second paramedic asked of the crowd:

"Does anyone know this man?"

No one responded at first, then a voice came from in back. "His name's Ben Weinstein."

"Do you know his medical history?"

"No," came from the faceless voice.

The paramedic remarked to his partner: "Let's get him in the truck."

They shifted the body onto the stretcher and the first paramedic barked to the crowd:

"Out of the way!"

After watching the paramedics leave, many in the elderly crowd remained fixed in their places.

From their expressions, Earl thought a few of them were visualizing themselves on the stretcher. A woman asked of no one in particular:

"Did he live here?"

Several persons agreed that the unconscious man wasn't a resident of the Hudson House. Earl heard another state: "I think he runs a little shoe store somewhere nearby."

The gathering broke up ... and Earl the Whirl began his search.

When Mr Weinstein had not returned after 45 minutes, Deuce found a key in the cash register, locked the door, and ran to the corner drug store. Rushing inside, he asked of the nearest employee:

"Where's your pay phone?"

Pointing to the rear of the store, the employee told him: "It's out of order though."

Deuce hurriedly checked all the aisles before going outside. On the corner, he checked the streets in each direction, then walked back to the shoe store.

At noon, business in the store was so busy that Deuce had little time to worry about Mr Weinstein. Within an hour, he'd sold eight pairs of shoes and was listening to his next customer repeat:

"Tommy-be-good!"

The object of her attention was a hyper 5-year-old who was yanking boxes off shelves faster than Deuce could replace them. Collaring her child, the mother dragged the boy into a chair and sat beside him.

Earl the Whirl --- having watched from the window for a minute --- entered the store.

Tucking a loose strand of hair over her ear,

the harried mother announced: "I'd like a pair of shoes like those he has on ... in the next larger size."

The 5-year-old, idle for a few seconds, made his move. Jumping out of his chair, he was a step away when his mother hollered:

"TOMMY-BE-GOOD!"

She grabbed a handful of shirt. Tommy stiffened like a collared cat as his mother pulled him silently back into his chair.

"Tommy-be-good," rattled the mother again, accentuating her words with a sharp tug of the shirt.

Undaunted, Tommy grasped the arms of the chair and strained forward while his mother held onto the shirt.

Deuce positioned a stool before the boy, sat down, and reached to take off the child's left shoe.

The shoe circled away.

Deuce easily caught it and began untying the laces. They were half-undone when the shoe jerked sideways and knotted the laces. As Deuce leaned closer to pick the knot, the child reversed his forward pull on the chair and swung his other shoe upward ... clipping Deuce's hand.

Massaging his hand, Deuce gave the mother a pained expression. While fumbling for her son's shirt, she had missed the kick.

Both shoes circled menacingly now.

Grabbing the left shoe, Deuce tried pulling it off without untying its lace. Between struggling with the shoe and dodging the other one, the first shoe came loose and landed several chairs away.

Confident of his technique now, Deuce leaned forward in pursuit of the right shoe. In seeming defeat, the 5-year-old stopped fidgeting.

Deuce took the right shoe, too ... in the eye.

Stunned, he reeled back on his stool.

The woman reached out to Deuce and lamely

offered: "I'm sorry. Tommy *didn't mean* to hurt you."

Earl the Whirl, with the first flying shoe in hand, approached the seated trio. Working a toothpick to the corner to his mouth, he graciously spoke.

"Folks, may I make a suggestion?"

The mother and Deuce looked up, while the triumphant brat sneered at the intruder. With a friendly grin, Earl removed the laces from the shoe and offered them to Deuce.

"Why not tie one foot to the chair?"

Deuce promptly reached for the laces and turned to the mother. "Would you please hold onto his foot with the shoe?"

When she did so, Deuce concentrated on the other kicking foot. Snaring it, he tied it to a chair leg. The child whimpered in defeat as Deuce then removed the right shoe and went in search of a match. By the time he returned, the child had begun to bawl. To reduce the crying, Deuce told the boy:

"Promise to hold still, and I'll untie you."

Instant quiet.

Keeping his head a safe distance away, Deuce warily untied the left foot from the chair and fitted a new shoe to it. The child remained relatively still as Deuce shifted to the right foot and fitted its shoe.

Tommy-be-good was nearing his limit.

As Deuce finished tying the last lace, the left shoe broke sharply inside --- trying to catch Deuce's hand in between the shoes.

Swiftly dropping his hand, Deuce watched Tommy's ankles smash together.

Squeals of genuine pain filled the store.

Deuce glanced up at the mother. "He kicked himself, lady."

She scowled back. "Do they fit?"

Deuce fumbled at the shoes until he had one in each hand. Pressing their toes, he told her: "They fit fine."

The mother tested the toes herself.

"Tommy-be-good," she sweetly implored. "Stand up and walk in your new shoes."

Deuce came off his stool and cautiously moved away.

Pushing himself out of his chair, the 5-year-old took several short steps. As he moved in a widening circle, his mother announced: "We'll take them."

Deuce smiled in relief at the woman, giving her child a third opening. The stiff toe of a new shoe bit into Deuce's shin like a chisel.

"Owww!" yelped Deuce, jumping backward as the child rushed forward to deliver another shot. Deuce cupped the brat's head with a hand and, using a stiff arm, kept him at bay.

"Tommy-be-good," said his mother with little concern, thinking the score had evened.

In frustration, the 5-year-old crouched lower to aim a kick and lost his balance in the process. He fell hard to the carpet...with renewed wailing.

Deuce placed the old shoes in an empty box and raised his voice to be heard over the din. "The shoes are $19.95."

The woman followed him to the cash register, leaving her son where he'd fallen. After paying for the shoes, she said:

"I don't want Tommy to scuff up his new shoes on the way home. Would you mind changing them?"

Deuce stared at her in disbelief, wondering why she didn't change them herself. He started to suggest the same ... and, in his delay, saw *his opening.*

"Sure," grinned Deuce.

As she dragged her child into a chair, Deuce

folded a piece of wrapping paper into a wad and slipped it inside the toe of one of the old shoes.

This time, he didn't bother untying the new shoes before pulling them off the boy's feet. However, he did use the laces again to tie a foot to the chair. Trapping the free foot between his knees, Deuce fitted the first old shoe.

Untying the second foot, Deuce took out his shoe horn. He placed it inside the heel of the second shoe before jamming the boy's foot home.

"Tommy-be-good!" alternated with new howls of the brat.

Ignoring her hobbling son's cries of protest, the mother towed him out the door.

Deuce closed the cash register with a satisfied smirk, then bent over to place the twenty dollar bill he'd received inside his stocking. When he came up, Earl the Whirl was examining a shoe display rack. The boy came around the counter and spoke in a complimentary tone.

That was a good idea to tie the foot."

Earl slyly smiled as he replaced a shoe on its stand. "It was a *better* idea to stick the paper in his shoe."

Deuce grinned back. "What type of shoes are you looking for?"

"Actually, I'm looking for my uncle, Ben Weinstein." The con man pulled an ivory toothpick from his breast pocket and placed it between his teeth. "Is he expected back soon?"

"He's ... uhh ..." faltered Deuce. "I don't know."

"Well, if you don't mind," Earl said pleasantly, "I'll wait for him." He removed his Panama hat and sat down.

7

Black Satin Pumps

The yipping of a small dog announced the next customer. A white toy poodle, wearing a pink bow, pranced into the store on a long rhinestone leash ... followed by a puffing woman. Her hot-pink tennis shoes paced with a skip as she came around and through the door.
"Co--pa--ce--tic."
Earl the Whirl drew the word out under his breath as he stood to measure the woman.
Oversized, gold-glazed sunglasses dominated the tanned skin of her cheery face. Platinum-blonde hair was coiled over her head and crowned by a Turkish fez, decorated with silk flowers. Earl accurately judged the petite woman to be in her mid-fifties and was pleased to note the cut of her pink short-skirted suit. A wide, gold belt was cinched tight and high to emphasize her generous figure.

Pretty as a peach, he mused, and ready for plucking. His eyes riveted on the curved seams of her outfit, studying whether it was hand-tailored, therefore imported and expensive. As she marched up to him, Earl decided it was.

Stopping a scant foot away from Earl, she fixed the distracted man with an engaging smile.

Earl --- intimidated by her nearness --- found himself leaning backward. He studied her unlined face and supposed she had been a stunning beauty in her time. Still is, Earl told himself.

"Sir"--- she spoke with a touch of a British accent ---"do you carry black satin pumps?"

Stepping back to better judge the woman's hourglass figure, Earl scanned her well-tanned legs. When his eyes arrived at the hot-pink tennis shoes, Earl drew himself up and affected a slight Continental accent himself.

"Of course, madam. Size five ... I presume."

"Six," she bubbled sweetly.

"Please have a seat" ---Earl half-bowed--- "while I check our inventory."

Earl placed a hand on Deuce's shoulder and led the boy to the rear. "Let me wait on her," whispered the con man, "and I'll give you a buck."

Seeing no harm to his benefit, Deuce nodded agreement.

"What's a pump?" asked Earl.

Deuce scrunched up his face. "I think she wants heels."

"Do you have any in black satin?"

"Pointed toes or rounded?" asked the boy. "High heels or low?"

"I don't know," said Earl. "Bring everything."

The boy loaded up Earl first, then gave himself an armload. They returned to find the pink lady on hands and knees, her head under a chair, trying to untangle her dog's leash from the chair legs.

"Madam," prompted Earl, "my assistant would be pleased to tend your poodle."

Her head came out from under the chair, the fez slightly off-center.

"You're so kind," she gushed and handed the leash to the boy. "Her name is Trixie."

Deuce knelt beside the dog, switching his hold on the leash to the opposite end by the dog's collar. He easily pulled the rest of the leash through the chair legs. This was lost on the woman, who was rising with Earl's helping hand.

"Why, thank you," she murmured at the courtesy.

His eyes were fixed on a glowing emerald ring, which caused the con man to hesitate in releasing her hand. A jumbo sapphire set in gold glittered on another finger.

As he let go, she winked at his wide-eyed expression. "Lovely, aren't they?"

Earl felt the fool. *You turkey!* he told himself. *Don't blow this one.*

For an instant, he wondered if he was getting too old to play the game.

"Gifts from my husband," she offered, seeing how interested he was in the rings.

He had been ... till she spoke.

Noting his fallen expression, she added: "My *late* husband."

His interest renewed, Earl glanced at her left hand. It was ringless. With a polished manner, he waved her into a chair.

"We have your shoes, madam."

Sitting before her on a stool, Earl opened the first box and removed a pair of black satin heels.

"Those aren't pumps," she mildly observed. "They have *straps*."

Earl the Whirl handed the box to Deuce and spoke as if the boy should have known better: "These aren't pumps."

The con man carefully inspected the shoes in the other boxes to assure they were strapless before offering them. After the woman had narrowed her choices to three pairs, she fitted them several times, before rising to test them.

With the first pair, she began to hum "La Cucaracha" as her feet slipped into a cha-cha.

Earl moved back, impressed by her effortless motion. After a few seconds, she said, "Too tight," and sat down to kick off the heels. Before Earl could assist, she had the next pair on and again stood. Humming a bit faster, she stepped into a brief samba, letting her body swing to the Latin beat. Her eyes had closed dream-like.

What a tigress, mused Earl.

When she re-opened her eyes and moved toward a chair, Earl quickly knelt to fit the final pair.

This time---keeping her eyes on Earl--she extended her hands before her, and let both arms and body flow into a smooth rumba. Her hips swayed, captivating her small audience.

Mercy! mused Earl. He'd never seen a woman move with such grace...or look more attractive in a dance. Her two-step twirls were flawless.

Earl lightly clapped his hands.

With an appreciative smile, she halted and eased back into her chair.

"I just can't decide which ones to get!" she exclaimed in a helpless tone.

The woman extended her legs out to better view her shoes, then asked:

"Which do you like?"

Earl, hypnotized by the well-defined muscles of her legs, replied:

"Both." Each leg looked fine to him.

"Both?" she grinned, enjoying the man's confusion.

Earl the Whirl blinked, trying to recall the question. He stammered: "Uh...let me see the other pair again."

Following more presentations of the beautifully tanned legs, Earl selected the last pair of heels. They had the tallest spikes.

"Those are my favorites, too," confirmed the pink lady, gratefully reaching over to pat his knee. "I'll take them."

After her tennis shoes were on again, she turned to Deuce sitting nearby with Trixie. The boy scratched at the chin of the poodle, which playfully nipped at his fingers. It had wound its leash around his chair this time.

"Well, young man...looks like Trixie's made a new friend."

Standing and lifting his chair up, Deuce instantly freed the dog and handed over the leash.

"How clever," remarked the pink lady, opening her handbag and removing a brocaded coin purse. She pulled out a hundred-dollar bill and started to offer it to Earl. "My goodness! I haven't even asked the price."

Earl checked the shoebox. "Thirty-nine, ninety-five, madam."

She pressed the bill into his hand.

"I'll prepare a receipt," said Earl. He gave the money to Deuce and asked: "Would you make change for this?"

The boy started to reach into the stocking of his right foot, but thought better. Going to the cash register, he took out a few ones and ducked behind the beaded curtain before removing the money cache from his sock. He counted out the necessary change, then totalled the remainder and returned to the register. Earl the Whirl was still filling out a receipt.

"Your address, Miss Toogood?"

Deuce placed the change on the counter, thinking it strange the man asked for an address. Mr Weinstein had never asked for one.

"I'm at the U.S. Grant Hotel for the holidays," she revealed. "Suite 322."

Earl scribbled this on the receipt and handed over the change. "What, may I ask," he casually inquired, "is the occasion for these fine shoes?"

"The Grant's having a Christmas dance tonight," she warmly replied, "and I've worn out the heels of my other dancing shoes."

Earl handed over the boxed pumps. "I'm certain you'll have many partners with these shoes, Miss Toogood."

The pink lady glowed. *"I love to dance.* Do you?"

Earl the Whirl drew himself up. "I was born dancing."

"Me, too," she responded. Turning to leave, the woman paused and looked back at Earl in a serious manner. "We're permitted to invite guests. Would you like to come?"

The con man, who already planned to attend, nodded. "I'd be delighted!"

"Begins at eight-thirty ... in the Crystal Ballroom," she said with a wink. Revolving twice to unwind the rhinestone leash from her ankles, the pink lady started toward the door.

Earl watched as the woman began to skip like a playful child. At the store's entrance she suddenly spun about.

"My goodness," she called out. "I don't know *your* name."

"Earl ... Earl Weinstein, at your service," he half-bowed.

She reflected on the name a moment. "Please call me, Tanya."

Waving, she passed out of sight.

"Now, there's one fine lady," commented Earl.

Deuce held out his palm. "One dollar, mister."

The con man eyed the boy a moment before reaching into his sports jacket. Pulling out two silver dollars, Earl asked: "What's your name, son?"

The boy told him.

"Tell you what, Deuce. How'd you like to go double or nothing?"

The man held out the coins in his palms, displaying a heads-up in his right hand and a tails in the other.

"You call the flip," Earl coaxed, "and they're both yours."

Eyeballing easy money, Deuce nodded.

"What's it going to be?" prompted Earl.

"Heads."

The con man flipped the coin in his left hand and let it fall to the floor. The coin bounced and settled.

"Tails," he observed and scooped up the double-tailed coin.

Sitting down, Earl promptly changed the subject. "Why'd you go behind the curtain to make change for the lady?"

Deuce kept steady eye contact with Earl as he searched for a misleading reply. When nothing came, he tried the truth.

"Mr Weinstein keeps mostly ones in the register. I had to go to the bathroom to get larger bills."

Earl checked his watch. "When does my uncle normally close shop?"

Deuce shrugged, then said: "The front door has a sign." He went to it and called back: "Five o'clock."

"It's five-ten now," replied Earl, glancing around. "If you want to go, I'll watch the store until he returns." With that, the con man took a chair near the counter.

Deuce went to the store's entrance again and looked down both ends of the street. Earlier, in the bathroom, he'd counted $231 after making change for the hundred-dollar bill; and now he debated whether to give Earl the money. It occurred to him that, if they closed the store, he wouldn't have to give up the money. Deuce came back to the counter.

"If you stay," began Deuce, "why don't we close up?"

"Good idea!" Earl hastily agreed.

"There's a door key in the register," offered Deuce. "Hit double-00 to open it. Tell Mr Weinstein I'll be back at ten tomorrow."

The boy hurried out, going in the direction of the corner drugstore.

When he'd locked the door, Earl moved fast. After checking the obvious places in the bathroom, he was pulling back its carpet when he heard a rapping at the store front. Coming to the beaded curtain, Earl spotted Deuce staring though the glass door. The con man went to open it.

"I forgot something," explained Deuce, marching to the rear.

The con man lagged behind. When Deuce ducked under the counter, Earl made a mental note to check there, too. Coming up with a book and the paper bag holding his clothes, Deuce went behind the curtain to change clothes.

"I was looking for some aspirin," Earl said at the curtain. "Do you know where my uncle keeps it?"

"No," Deuce replied.

Concerned the boy might notice the items stacked in the sink, Earl added: "I checked the bathroom."

Deuce came through the curtain wearing his shoeshining outfit. "I'm going to the drugstore to check again on your uncle. Do you want me to bring back some aspirin?"

Struck by the boy's kindness, Earl paused before saying: "Don't bother. But please let me know if you find out anything about my uncle."

Deuce left again and Earl resumed his search. After lifting the carpet from the bathroom floor, raising the cabinet mirror off its hinges, and checking for hollow partitions in the sink console, he switched his attention to the cash register and its counter. Three-quarters of an hour after Deuce left, the con man looked at his watch.

"Come on, Earl baby!" he exclaimed. "Get a move on!"

On the way back to the Hudson House, he stopped at a men's clothing store and a small grocery. At the first stop, he found a silk handkerchief in radiant pink; and, at the second, a treat for Trixie.

Later--- after taking a nap ---Earl the Whirl stood before the dresser's mirror in his room and edged a bit more of the pink handkerchief from his breast pocket. He intended to be the center of attention tonight...as far as the women were concerned. Even the men would stare at the *Miami Ice*---his term for the cream-colored silk suit he now wore.

Stretching his hand under the dresser, Earl brought out a small, black velvet box. He shook its contents like a pair of dice and, hearing its contents, dropped the box inside a pocket of his jacket.

On the street again, Earl headed north up 6th Avenue, in the opposite direction of the U.S.

Grant. When the street became steeper, he paused to catch his breath and admire the tower of the El Cortez Hotel.

At the reception desk of the El Cortez, Earl asked for the floor of its tower restaurant. Moments later, he stepped out of the elevator directly into The Condor.

An overflow of guests crowded around the wraparound bar at the center of the restaurant. After speaking briefly with the headwaiter and pressing a five-dollar bill into the man's hand, Earl walked back down the hill...arriving at the U.S. Grant a few minutes before eight-thirty.

8

The Condor

For some years after a multi-million dollar restoration in the 1980s, the U.S. Grant Hotel regained the splendor and popularity it'd known when the son of the general/president opened its doors in 1910. But the new owners had forgotten the hard lesson learned by the son of the Civil War President. Most of San Diego's visitors preferred to stay nearer its beaches. Eventually, the U.S. Grant reverted to its former clientele ... although this time it was a more well-to-do segment of the downtown retirement community.

At eight-thirty, Earl poked his head inside the ballroom. It was crowded already. Most of the women and men were separated --- the women sitting along the perimeter tables just as they'd stationed themselves in their teens. Half as many men stood in clusters on the dance floor ... nursing drinks.

A few couples --- serene in their security --- sat together.

Taking in the well-dressed women, Earl the Whirl almost regretted he'd be missing "the stalk," as he termed it. Early in the evening, it was his habit to choose a new partner with each dance, in order to find the best prospects before spending money on their drinks.

Something touched his elbow, delivering an electric shock which shivered Earl's entire body. He twisted around, off-balance.

The pink lady wore no pink tonight.

Tanya's platinum blonde tresses curled around bare shoulders, framing a wide expanse of smooth skin. His eyes followed a strand of milky pearls to the wine-red chiffon of her strapless dress.

"Whoops!" she exclaimed. "I didn't mean to jolt you."

In the mellowed light, the glamorous woman reminded Earl of a movie star, though he could not pinpoint which one. The band began a waltz, and Tanya fitted her arm within his.

"Shall we make our entrance?" she suggested.

Immensely proud to be escorting such a gorgeous woman, Earl promenaded Tanya to the center of the ballroom before twirling her into the three-step tempo. After their first circle of the dance floor, he told her:

"You trip the light fantastic!"

"And you" ---she leaned back on his arm--- "lead magnificently."

Earl returned her warm smile. They spoke sparingly; and, as was his custom, Earl let his partner determine the closeness between them... having found this distance narrowed sooner when he displayed disinterest. With the second slow dance of the evening, Earl was conscious of the attention he imagined they received from others in the ballroom.

Earl seldom observed a man who he thought danced better than himself, and tonight Earl felt he had the perfect partner. When the band began a tango, Earl locked his head like a professional, letting his gaze sweep the ballroom in a blur.

At the conclusion of the tango, Earl noted a moist glow on Tanya's forehead.

"Would you like to rest?" he inquired.

The band began a slow melody.

"After this one," Tanya softly said. Not waiting for his response, she placed a hand on his shoulder and led him into the rhythm.

What's happening? Earl wondered. I'm letting her lead me. Who is this woman? As he struggled to maintain a modest interval, Tanya steadily danced closer. When the band took a break, Earl and Tanya wandered hand-in-hand in search of a vacant table. Unable to find one, they were on the edge of the dance floor when Tanya took one of his hands in both of hers.

"Earl," she crinkled her eyes at him, "you are the finest partner I've ever romanc---"

Tanya caught herself. "---danced with."

His eyes widening, Earl stared through her, thinking that's *my line*.

Bringing his hand to her cheek, Tanya said: "I didn't mean to embarrass you."

"No ... no ... not at all," sputtered Earl, even more unnerved by the touch of her warm skin. Casting his eyes aside, he spoke again, too hastily to sound sincere. "You're a fine dancer, too."

It was the normal response to the line she'd just taken from him. Frowning at the crowded ballroom, Earl commented:

"This place is certainly popular."

"And stuffy," added Tanya at the cigarette haze over the ballroom.

Earl took the cue. "I know a place nearby where the air's much better."

"How far?" she asked.

"A few blocks north," he said. "Only a minute by taxi."

"Let's go."

Though The Condor bustled with its night crowd, the headwaiter promptly recognized the man in the cream-colored suit.

"Good evening, sir ... madam," he elegantly intoned.

"Evening, William." replied Earl. "We'd like a west view."

The headwaiter winked and ushered them to a table at the previously-requested corner of the open-air terrace.

At their table, Earl waited behind Tanya's chair as she remained standing, taking in the view. The lighted cross over La Jolla was clearly visible in the dark sky. Tanya's gaze swept past the islands of Mission Bay, along the imposing outlines of two aircraft carriers across the harbor, and southward to the blinking lights of Mexico.

Sitting, she asked: "Do you come here often?"

"Occasionally," he offered.

A waiter appeared. Tanya ordered a pineapple margarita and raised an eyebrow when Earl asked for a Perrier and lime.

"You don't drink?" she asked.

Not when I'm working, thought Earl, and he said:

"Not when I'm thinking."

Tanya lightly laughed. "Of what are you thinking?"

"Today."

The word was spoken in a perfect monotone. Earl watched her cheerful expression turn serious.

"I don't understand," said Tanya.

"This is the day"---Earl dramatically paused---"we met."

She cocked her head to one side.

Earl the Whirl continued. "I want to remember everything about today. The way you skipped into the store, the first words you spoke to me, what you wore ... everything."

Tanya extended a hand to place it over his.

He wrinkled his brow. "I've been meaning to ask --- why do you skip?"

She paused thoughtfully. "I suppose for the reactions. People smile at me, they become friendly. Sometimes, they even start skipping themselves."

"I'll have to try it," he told her.

"And, it's great for my legs!" she added with enthusiasm.

He returned her broad smile and reached for a menu. "I haven't eaten since breakfast. Will you dine with me?"

Tanya withdrew her hand and replied in a subdued voice. "Something light."

Earl looked over the menu. "I'd suggest the Chicken Cordon Bleu or the Monte Cristo."

"Will you help me with the Monte Cristo?"

"If you'll share the Cordon Bleu with me," he smiled.

Her eyes floated skyward and came back down. "We sound like lovers."

Surprised at the comment, Earl paused before nodding. "Maybe, we were."

"Were?"

"In a past life," he continued.

"You believe in reincarnation?"

"Most of the time ... no." Earl leaned forward. "But ever since your pink mirage entered the store today, I'm certain I've seen you before."

It was a routine line. In its calculated and casual delivery, Earl the Whirl missed a momentary alert that flashed in the woman's eyes.

Tanya's face turned dreamy. "I feel the same. As if I've always known of your existence ... without actually knowing you."

She paused, grinning helplessly. "It gets confusing."

Earl thought to himself, it's never been this ideal. He studied Tanya's face and saw only the beguiling smile. Seldom had a woman been attracted to him so quickly. And that she was as lovely as this was hard to believe.

After the waiter returned with drinks and their dinners were ordered, Earl decided he could think better on his feet.

"Hey!" he exclaimed. "We came here to dance."

Taking a healthy swallow of her margarita, Tanya popped up. On the crowded dance floor, Earl found it impossible to maintain a discreet distance between them. Tanya soon placed her cheek on his shoulder and Earl folded his head over hers before half-closing his eyes. It was easier to dream than to think.

He saw himself in a forest where they strolled together. A woman skipped ahead of him, and he ran blindly after her. She kept just beyond his outstretched hand. Then, she stopped. And his hand went through her fading image.

Earl opened his eyes. They were the only ones left on the dance floor. The music had ended.

Behind them, a growing cheer came from the patrons of The Condor. Earl thought the acclaim was for how well they'd danced, but he and Tanya turned and saw a number of guests waving napkins in the opposite direction.

"Goodness!" uttered Tanya. "What is that?"

A majestic plane, with blinding beams, had appeared in the eastern sky.

As the circling beams came even with the restaurant, lights of the city illuminated the giant fuselage and silver wings of a Boeing 747 ... no more than 250 yards distant. The jumbo-jet, with a wing-span of 73 yards, dwarfed the tower of the El Cortez ... yet there'd been no warning of its approach.

The dull roar of the plane's muted engines built for a few seconds, then waned as the 747 coasted toward a runway of Lindbergh Field 2,500 yards away.

She gaped after the aircraft. "I thought that was a UFO."

"They call this The Condor," explained Earl, "because planes swoop down on it like a giant bird."

Tanya pulled him to their table where they watched the flashing lights of the great plane magically descend to the runway of the airport.

9

A Midnight Snack

While sharing dinners, Earl and Tanya explored each other's past.

Tanya revealed she'd lost her husband --- an Australian oil executive --- to a plane accident three years previously, had no children, and alternated between condominiums in Santa Barbara and Palm Springs ... with brief sojourns to San Diego.

Earl described an early retirement after the sale of a chain of shoe stores in Chicago ... in addition to making up a divorce 15 years earlier. The con man also expressed an intention to stay in California permanently, as he planned to open a shoestore in San Diego to complement his uncle's store.

On the dance floor again, they moved as one. Craning his head away from her, Earl said: "I miss looking at you ... when we're so near."

Tanya's face brightened and she snuggled even closer. When they returned to their table, he silently reached across to hold her hands.

"Tanya, I could dance with you every night of my life."

Intermingling her fingers with his, she crinkled her eyes in a smile. "That would please me."

Earl caressed each of her fingers, one by one ... as if thinking deeply. He was: for he found himself almost believing his words this time.

Having made his sentimental pause long enough, he reached into his jacket and brought forth the small black velvet box. Earl placed it mid-table.

"Please open it," he prompted her.

Finding a silver ring with a half-carat clear stone mounted inside, she picked it out.

"This sparkles like a diamond!" she exclaimed.

"It has been in my family for many years," Earl told her. "I want you to have it ... to celebrate our meeting today."

"Who did it belong to?" asked Tanya.

"My mother."

"This must be quite precious to you," said Tanya, turning the ring over in her fingers before looking to Earl. "I can't accept it."

He gave his standard reply to the standard refusal.

"My mother---God rest her soul---had many rings," smiled the con man, nodding his head. "I'm certain she would have approved of your having this one."

"Thank you," Tanya began, "but---"

"Tis the season for giving," he interrupted.

Before she could respond, Earl added: "Please take it tonight as a token of our friendship. We can always find another ring tomorrow."

The line worked most of the time, as it did now. In fact, he had purchased the ring in a second-hand store for less than twenty dollars.

Earl reached over and gently slid the zircon onto the ring finger of the woman's right hand.

On the next day, he would say nothing about finding another ring ... and rarely would the woman bring the matter up again either.

Tanya's eyes had misted over. They went from Earl...to the ring...and back to him. Abruptly, she stood. Coming around the table, she leaned over and touched his lips briefly with hers.

"Bless you," she said.

Earl thought the salty margarita flavor mixed well with her lipstick. Yet, the intimacy saddened the man and he dropped his eyes.

Looking into her softly glowing face, Earl the Whirl had finally remembered who Tanya reminded him of. It was a Ginger Rogers movie poster of a half-century earlier...and he recalled the fantasies of his boyhood.

With eight brothers and sisters in a basement flat of Brooklyn, there had been few illusions in Earl's home. Both parents worked to barely support their too-large family. Schooling for the children ended at the age of 13, when they too were sent out to work. Four years of toiling from dawn to dusk as a delivery boy and loading trucks had cured Earl of the practice of physical labor.

During those years of drudgery, he would often sneak into movie theaters...and transport himself into their make-believe worlds of adventure, wealth, and happiness. At 17, he'd left home in order to keep his earnings. With a quick mind, Earl soon learned the edge to the games of chance played in the alleys and poolhalls. And his winnings paid for brief flings into the lifestyles of his Hollywood idols.

Earl had pursued the lavish dream all his life ... but he had taken too many short-cuts along the way.

As a result, he'd spent a third of his adult life as the guest of various houses of detention. Just paying my dues, Earl had told the other con men he met in prison. He found the hardest part was not the time spent behind bars ... it was picking up the pieces afterwards. Vague and overdue explanations for his unexplained and prolonged absences were never sufficient to keep friends ... of either sex.

Earl raised his eyes only high enough to take in Tanya's lovely shoulders. And this sweet woman, he reflected, would not even become a friend.

As she moved to sit again, Earl could stand his gloomy feelings no longer and came to his feet.

"May we dance again," he asked.

They danced under the Christmas stars until the band signed off. In the taxi, Tanya---after commenting on the cool air---cuddled up to Earl for warmth.

"This is one of the most wonderful evenings of my life," she whispered.

Earl gave her a short hug. "For me, too."

At the U.S. Grant, they proceeded through the lobby and up the elevator, both wondering what the other would do when they arrived at her door.

At Suite 322, Tanya handed the key to Earl. Opening the door, he replaced the key in her hand.

The silence ended with the yipping of Trixie, who'd awakened at the click of the lock. The toy poodle calmed at the sight of its mistress, but circled Earl ... sniffing anxiously at the cuffs of his trousers.

"Trixie, what's come over you?" posed Tanya.

Earl the Whirl bent over to extract something from a pants cuff and offered it to the dog. Trixie immediately took the dog cookie from his fingers.

"She's just hungry for a midnight snack," said Earl, offering Trixie more.

"You charm everyone!" Tanya laughed. "Come in, and I'll fix *you* a snack, too."

Tanya pushed her door open wide. Earl took in the living room of the luxurious suite. Fresh fruit overflowed a large bowl on a coffee table, and a wet bar stood beside the sliding door of a balcony.

He held back. "I'm a bit old-fashioned."

"The night's young," she teased.

"You're special to me, Tanya." Earl had the weird feeling that, this time, he'd meant the words. That's no way to run a business, he silently criticized himself.

The delight on the woman's face began to dim.

Earl gave her an encouraging grin. "Would you accompany me on a harbor cruise tomorrow?"

Tanya's face relaxed into a smile. "I'd love to."

"Till then" ---he waxed poetic--- "may I kiss you again."

This time, after a lingering kiss, Earl had to catch his breath before speaking.

"Goodnight, lovely lady."

Tanya gave him a final peck on the cheek. "Goodnight, darling."

At the elevator, Earl pivoted and they waved goodbye.

As he exited the holiday-decorated lobby of the U.S. Grant, he disgustedly muttered: "Business!"

❄ **Part Two** ❄

Two Days Till Christmas

Characters & *Props* for Part Two*

10   Deuce - *spring grip, book*
     Earl the Whirl - *briefcase with jewelry box
               inside(cigar-box size)*
     White-Haired Lady
     Younger Woman
     Maria

11   Deuce - *shoeboxes(a lot)*
     Maria
     Spike
     Cruz
     Joe
     Earl the Whirl - *deck of ards, play money*

12   Earl the Whirl
     Perfect Pear (lady customer) - *small armchair*

13   Deuce - *deck of cards, play money*
     Maria
     Earl the Whirl

14   Earl the Whirl
     Tanya Toogood

*assign someone to read the non-conversation and another for the props.

10

"Feed The Hungry Hunter"

Deuce's left hand worked his spring-grip while he read in the shade of the shoe store's entrance.
At the same time, he kept a watchful eye on the woman beside him. She was studying shoes in the window display. Several other persons also had stopped to browse at the window since he'd arrived a half-hour earlier.
The boy was certain he could've made sales to some of the window-shoppers. He was tempted to ask the woman to wait, explaining the store would open shortly. In his scruffy shoeshining outfit though, Deuce decided she wouldn't pay any attention to him, and he returned to his book.
At the end of each page, Deuce switched the spring-grip to the other hand and checked the sidewalk in both directions. He was looking for a

slow-moving, slight figure in grey. Consequently, the man carrying a briefcase and wearing a blue-and-cream jacket escaped his notice until the last moment. Earl the Whirl spoke in a jocular note.

"Morning, my boy!"

Earl fitted the key to the door as Deuce asked:

"Did Mr Weinstein come back last night?"

"I don't know." Earl pretended concern. "I only waited around an hour."

On the chance the storeowner was in back, Deuce hurried to the beaded curtain and called out in the dark.

"Mr Weinstein!"

There was no response.

Having followed Deuce, Earl asked him: "Did you learn anything down at the drugstore?"

Deuce shook his head. "They didn't remember seeing him."

A man in a business suit walked in and the boy snatched the grocery bag of clothes from under the counter.

"I've got to change," explained Deuce, going behind the curtain.

"I can handle the customer," Earl offered. When Deuce emerged in white shirt and brown trousers, Earl had already sold the man a pair of loafers out of the display window. As the customer left, the boy placed the money in the cash register.

"Deuce, how long have you been selling shoes here?" Earl's tone was friendly.

Trying to look busy counting change at the register, Deuce considered his answer. To say "a few days" might encourage the relative to take over. He gave a bothered reply.

"For a while."

Earl's tone turned serious. "What's for a while?"

"Coupla weeks," offered Deuce, glancing up for a moment.

The curiosity on the man's face turned to a tight grin as Earl lifted his briefcase onto the counter and released its catches. Before opening it, he checked the front door. A white-haired lady walked into the store, followed by a well-dressed, younger woman. The con man snapped the catches of his briefcase shut and set it under the counter as Deuce approached the first customer.

While the boy devoted his attention to the older woman who'd entered first, the other one impatiently paced nearby holding a pair of tennis shoes from a display rack.

As Deuce brought shoes to the elderly lady, she carefully inspected each pair for flaws, rejecting everything Deuce presented to her.

After five minutes of being ignored, the second woman dropped the tennis shoes on a chair and walked out.

A few minutes later, the white-haired woman came to her feet --- still not having tried on anything.

"Young man, they don't make shoes the way the used to." With that, she left the store.

In a sullen mood, Deuce shelved the accumulated boxes.

Earl waited until all the boxes were put away before speaking.

"You have to feed the hungry hunter, my boy."

Confused, Deuce frowned at the con man.

"The next time you have two customers," Earl goodnaturedly offered, "don't zero in on either one so fast. Wait until you know which is the best bet."

"How do you do that?" Deuce grudgingly inquired.

"Easy," grinned Earl. "Get them to commit themselves. Ask what they're looking for? ...what style they prefer? ...what size they wear? Anything that will narrow their interests down."

Deuce sat on the stool next to the register.

"If you don't know what they're hunting for," continued Earl, "how in the world can you help them find it?"

The boy shrugged. "The old lady couldn't make up her mind."

The con man played with his mustache to hide a smirk. "That woman was paying you a social visit, Deuce. She was on her afternoon stroll and, most likely, felt like talking to someone."

Another businessman came in, and this time Deuce sold a pair of shoes, though the man hemmed and hawed at the last moment. Business picked up during the noon hour, and Earl volunteered to assist when necessary. Between locating shoes for Earl's customers and then his own, Deuce had sold three fewer pairs than his new assistant when the store finally emptied.

"You're a good salesman," Deuce said to the con man.

Tempted to correct the vast understatement, Earl instead said: "You're doing better, my boy. But if you want to keep up with me, you've got to sell *scarcer goods*."

Earl paused to let his words sink in. As he did so, he noticed that it was noon on the wall clock. Removing his watch, he adjusted its time by 21 minutes.

"When a customer appears to know which shoes they want," continued the con man, "and you have those shoes in front of them, tell them it's the last pair in the store."

Deuce questioned the advice with a sour look.

"And how do you know," added Earl, "that it *isn't* the last pair of shoes ... unless you spend a half hour double-checking?"

As Deuce listened, the words "for the sake of a bone" came to mind.

"That way," Earl continued, "you increase their desire for the shoes they're thinking of buying --- because they'll be afraid *somebody else* will walk in and buy them if they don't."

For the next hour, Deuce almost kept up with the con man in sales ... even though he only used the "scarcer goods" closing when he thought it true. After business slackened, Earl pulled out his briefcase and set it on the counter again. Releasing its catches, he spoke in a low voice.

"I'll show you why I came to see my uncle."

When Earl opened the small briefcase, Deuce saw only a round lacquered box within. Its lid was inlaid with mother-of-pearl in the form of a multi-colored peacock, with wings fully spread. When the man raised the lid, Deuce came nearer, his mouth agape.

An array of necklaces, bracelets, and rings filled the box to its brim.

"This is my uncle's inheritance," announced Earl, "from my father's estate."

Earl picked out a thick ring with a large, red stone and held it before the boy's eyes. In a hushed tone, he told Deuce: "This ruby was appraised at over two-thousand dollars." He handed it to Deuce who held it cupped in his palms like a thin-shelled egg.

"Someone's coming." Earl half-whispered and plucked the ring from the boy's hands. As Deuce turned, the con man palmed the ruby ring with the flesh of his thumb as he closed the briefcase.

Deuce recognized the new arrival and started around the counter. He didn't respond when Earl said: "I'm putting this in back."

Maria paused just inside the door. She wore a yellow jumpsuit that nicely accented her olive-toned skin. The red lipstick, violet eye shadow, and rose makeup over her cheekbones were as boldly applied as the day before.

"Can I try on the dancing shoes again?" she asked of Deuce.

Deuce walked toward Maria, acting as if he hadn't heard her words. He had and he hadn't. When he stood before her, putting his hands in his pockets, Maria sensed his nervousness and repeated her request.

"Sure," replied Deuce. He pivoted and headed for the back of the store, moving without direction. As hard as he tried, he couldn't remember where the red dancing shoes were. Deuce scanned the store at random.

"Didn't they come from over there?" called out Maria, pointing to a shelf Deuce had passed.

11

The Game's Called Monte

When Deuce found the box with Maria's shoes, she was already seated and removing a sandal. He sat before her as she released the straps of the other sandal. A timid smile played on her face when she looked up.

Deuce quickly dropped his eyes and set about fitting one of the red heels.

He noticed that her neatly manicured toenails were painted the same purple as the shadow over her eyes. When the other red heel was fitted, Deuce stood and uncertainly offered his hand.

Maria pushed herself up without assistance this time. Having practiced with her mother's heels, she wavered only a moment before assuming a poised stance.

When her eyes suddenly widened in alarm, Deuce looked to the front of the store with her. His gut tightened.

The All-American T-Team stood at the entrance. The white punk spoke.
"Hey, Short-stuff!" Spike called out mockingly. "How 'bout showing us some skids?"
Deuce glanced around for a weapon. There was only the stool at his feet.
Sauntering over to a shelf, Spike pulled out a box. After examining its contents, he lifted up a pair of tennis shoes and tossed them to the Latino.
"Cruz! This your size?"
The Latino caught one of the shoes in mid-air and flung it over his shoulder. "Wrong color."
Grabbing another box, Spike threw its shoes to the black punk. "You like these, Joe?"
Joe batted them away like balls. "Not my style, Spike."
"Hey, Short-stuff," Spike turned again to Deuce. "What kinda skids you got in this dump anyway?"
With an arm, the white youth swept an entire shelf clear. Kicking at the contents of the boxes, he shouted to his buddies: "Come on! If Short-stuff won't help us, we gotta help ourselves."
And he swept another shelf clear. As the boxes clattered to the floor, the two other punks headed for shelves.
"Wait a minute, boys."
The words came in a clear baritone from the back of the store.
The trio paused ... checking out the man leaning nonchalantly in the entry way by the beaded curtain. Earl the Whirl grinned as if he had been enjoying the show.
"Who are you?" snarled Spike.
Earl raised an eyebrow and calmly spoke. "Someone in need of protection."
"*Protection?*" questioned Spike.

Holding his smile, the con man came around the counter. As he neared the white youth, Earl drew his words out deliberate and slow.

"I was thinking of asking you for protection, Spike."

"Hey, man," sneered the punk, slightly unnerved by the con man's coolness. "What kinda talk is that?"

"Simple, my lad," Earl replied. "The store needs security. You know ... from kids who break windows, shoplift, loiter around --- that sort of thing."

A wicked grin distorted Spike's face. He glanced knowingly at the other two punks before coming back to Earl.

"So, what's it worth to yah, mister?"

Earl took his time looking over the intruders before responding. "How about five dollars every Monday?"

"*Come on!*" snorted Spike.

"I meant five dollars each," said Earl, adding: "And we'll throw in an extra five to you, Spike ... for supervision."

"Maybe me and you can do business, mister," nodded Spike. He twisted around to his buddies.

"Hey, whatsa matter, you jerks! Get them boxes back on shelves!"

"Don't worry about the boxes," countered Earl the Whirl. He addressed Deuce. "Son, why don't you get 20 dollars for our new friends?"

As Deuce passed him, Earl winked and whispered: "Only ones."

Removing dollar bills from the register, Deuce went behind the curtain. When he returned, Earl had gathered the three toughs at the counter.

"The game's called monte, boys." Earl the Whirl smoothly rotated a row of three face-down playing cards on the countertop. "You've heard of El Monte, east of LA? That's where this game started ... more than a hundred years ago. Choose either of the two aces, you lose."

Pick the lady" ---Earl turned over the queen of hearts--- "you win."

After moving the cards around at moderate speed, the man said: "Go ahead, Spike. Where's the lady."

The white punk tapped a card.

"Good eye," commented Earl, flipping it over to reveal the queen. As he held the card up, Earl bent a corner ... shielding it so only Spike noticed the crimp being made.

"Care to bet a dollar on your eye?" Earl asked him.

Spike reached inside his pants pocket. "Anytime, pal."

Earl raised a hand. "One moment, my lad." He turned to Deuce. "Have you got their fees?"

Deuce handed over 20 ones, then stood to the side with Maria to watch the card play.

After Earl counted out ten to Spike and five each to Cruz and Joe, he asked: "Now, what'll you bet?"

Spike threw a dollar down.

Earl the Whirl rotated the cards a bit faster this time, then stopped and gracefully spread his hands away from them. Spike instantly pointed to the left-hand card.

"Turn it over," Earl suggested.

The queen came up again.

Earl made a short grimace as he pulled out a silver money clip. Removing a dollar, he placed it on the counter and asked: "Want to double your bet?"

Spike did, and after he'd won again, Earl looked to the other punks. "You lads want to try your luck, too?"

Joe slapped two dollars down.

"Big spender," commented Earl as he spun the cards. When they stopped, Joe hesitated ... having no idea where the queen was. He touched the middle card.

"Sorry, Joe," said Earl, flipping over an ace.

Joe bet only a dollar on his second bet, and the con man slowed the cards to let him win.

When Cruz cautiously put a dollar down on his first bet, Earl again slowed the queen to keep it evident. But when the Latino doubled his next bet, the cards speeded up and he lost.

After another minute, Deuce decided to sort out the strewn contents of the shoeboxes thrown about the front of the store. Maria helped him, keeping the red heels on.

Within 15 minutes, Cruz and Joe had parted with their "protection" money ... and then some. Spike was ahead.

When his turn came around again, Spike threw three dollars on the counter. After the cards stopped, he leaned over to study them. The crimp was barely evident. Turning the queen over, Spike greedily took his winnings and announced:

"Five bucks this time."

When Earl halted the cards, Spike again bent over to locate the crimp. This time he found *two* cards with bent corners. The white punk looked to Earl for a hint, but the con man kept his eyes on the cards. Spike came lower to study the crimps, his nose nearly on the same level as the cards.

"You wanna magnifying glass?" taunted Cruz.

Clearly frustrated, Spike grabbed the middle card, bringing up an ace.

"You had a good streak," soothed Earl, turning the ace face-down again.

As Joe pushed in for a turn, Spike angrily protested. "Hold on! Let's change cards."

"Sure," agreed Earl with a casual smile. Locating the other two aces and a new queen, he removed them from the deck and again gave the last card a barely perceptible crimp. When Spike's turn came up, he spotted the single crimp and threw down five dollars.

The cards spun at a dazzling speed. When they stopped, Spike promptly turned over the card to his right.

"Ha!" he exclaimed. "Got the lady!"

Earl turned the queen back over. As he doled out five dollars, Earl told Spike: "You're winning all your friends' money."

"They're just a coupla birdbrains," Spike jeered. Counting out his stack of ones, Spike placed them on the countertop.

"There's $16. Spin 'em, mister!"

Earl started to rotate the cards.

"Wait!" yelled Spike. He pulled out his $10 *protection fee* and added it to the money pile.

The three cards spun in a blur. Whenever moving the queen, Earl placed his index finger on its crimp ... not stopping the rotation until friction between the countertop and the queen had ironed out the crimp. As the cards slowed, he put a slight crimp --- for insurance --- on one of the aces.

Spike stooped over again to check the three cards and saw only one with a bent corner. As he flipped it over, Spike confidently said: "Pay off, sucker!"

Cruz coarsely laughed at the faceup ace. "You're the *sucker*, Spike!"

Earl the Whirl sympathetically shook his head. He'd seen the shocked expression a thousand times. He awaited the explosion --- sometimes *that* was different.

The dumbfounded white punk turned the ace over and over, as if expecting a queen to show up on the other side. Pointing to a corner of the card, Spike angrily exclaimed:

"This card's got a wrinkle!"

Earl remained expressionless, waiting for the others to comment ... as he knew they would.

"So what," Cruz scoofed. "It's not the queen."

Joe snapped: "You blew it, dude."

Spike started to protest more, then stopped ...realizing to do so might reveal how he'd earlier won the money of his friends.

Earl, who had picked up the stack of dollars immediately after Spike turned over the ace, peeled off five bills and placed them on the counter before the still-seething white tough.

"Here's some beer money, lads."

The disgruntled Spike grabbed the dollars.

Earl continued. "I've got to get back to work now. Why don't you boys come back later in the week and we'll play some more?"

As the trio left, Earl hurriedly totalled the take. Pocketing six dollars, he waited till Deuce finished with a customer before handing him the balance.

"Here's your investment, son."

Deuce counted out the original 20 dollars and looked up curiously. "Did you trick them?"

Earl shook his head with a wry grin. "Actually, they tricked themselves. As the saying goes, you can't con an honest man."

"How'd you do it?" Deuce persisted. Maria, overhearing the conversation, had come to the side of Deuce.

Debating how much to reveal, Earl considered in his mind whether to make it seem more difficult.

"I appealed to their greed."

Deuce held a doubtful look.

"I'll show you," Earl offered. Taking the card deck from his pocket, he removed a queen and two aces and began rotating them face-down on the counter.

"First of all," began Earl, "let your players win a little in the beginning by not moving the cards too fast. It builds their confidence. And never ... *never* leave the queen in the middle when you're trying to win."

"Why not?" asked Deuce, keeping his eye on the shifting queen.

"Common sense, son. Most players --- when they've lost track of the queen --- usually choose the middle card. It's a compromise of their suspicions."

Earl the Whirl speeded up the cards as he continued. "The odds that a player will select the queen are one-in-three. By placing the queen to the side, you make the odds even worse."

The cards moved even faster on the countertop.

"Another tip --- keep up a running conversation with a player when a big bet is on. Ask them questions. It keeps them from concentrating."

The cards stopped.

"Where's the lady?" asked Earl.

Deuce stared at the cards. Even though he'd lost the queen, he knew his odds were one-in-two ... if the man had left the queen on the outside. Deuce tapped the card on his right.

"I forgot to mention" ---Earl chuckled as he flipped over the queen to the boy's left--- "to keep track of which hand your player uses to select his cards. Then ... when a big bet's on, leave the queen at his opposite hand."

After a pause, Earl added: "And keep the game short. Don't get greedy yourself. If you play too long, your customers" ---the con man caught himself--- 'I mean, players, tend to get confused and unpredictable."

The boy watched Earl scoop up the cards, thinking monte appeared a lot easier than kneeling on concrete shining shoes. He asked the man: "Do you always carry a deck of cards?"

"Doing card tricks is a hobby of mine," said Earl, riffling the cards from one hand to the other. "Want to see one?"

"Sure."

"I learned this one from a mathematician in Colorado," said Earl. "It's named: *You Call It*. Maria, I'm going to let you select a card from anywhere in the deck. Memorize it, and give it back to me...and while the cards are being shuffled, you decide whether it will re-appear as the first ... second ... or third card from the top of the deck."

Earl the Whirl neatly fanned the deck across the countertop, and Maria picked one. Secretively showing the ten-of-diamonds to Deuce, she placed it atop the deck Earl now held in his palm.

Shuffling the cards in the standard manner, Earl watched the boy and girl and made a private bet as to who would comment first. He lost.

"That's *easy*," Maria pointed to the deck. "You're keeping my card on top."

"Why do you say that?" asked Earl, switching his shuffling style to dropping the cards vertically into each other. After one vertical-shuffle, the con man dealt out the top ten cards faceup on the countertop.

"Where's your card?" inquired Earl with a friendly smile.

Maria shook her head. "It's gone."

Looking pleased, Earl recovered the face-up cards and placed them on top again. He did three rapid vertical-shuffles, then asked:

"Where would you like your card to be *now*, young lady?"

Maria looked to Deuce. When he shrugged, she said:

"The top card."

99

It was the selection made fully half the time, and Earl promptly placed the deck face-down. "See if you're right."

Reaching over to pick off the top card, Maria stared at it, then showed the card to Deuce.

"It's the ten," she whispered.

"How'd you do that?" asked Deuce.

"I'll do it again," said Earl. "This time, you pick the card."

After Deuce selected the three-of-hearts, Earl immediately started a vertical-shuffle. Deuce said his chosen card would be the second one from the top. Doing three more vertical-shuffles, Earl placed the deck on the counter.

The second card off the top of the deck was the three-of-hearts.

"Neat trick," commented Deuce, looking thoroughly confused.

Earl, appreciating the boy's compliment, told him: "Watch my shuffle, son."

Slower this time, he started his vertical-shuffle ... until Deuce realized Earl was pulling off only the very top and bottom cards with his right hand each time he split the deck. These two cards were then held in the man's lowered right hand as the other 50 cards were dropped in front or behind the two cards ... depending on whether Earl wanted to move the three-of-hearts to the cellar of the deck or back to the top.

"I got it," nodded Deuce. "Let me show Maria."

Handing the deck over, Earl told him: "If you get that trick down, I'll show you a few more."

The boy began practicing the vertical-shuffle.

Remembering a mystery of his own, Earl winked at Maria and said: "I'll watch for customers if you two want to go down to the drugstore for a soda."

Deuce spilled the cards on the floor at the man's suggestion. While Maria changed back into her sandals, Earl helped the boy pick up the cards. When they'd finished, Earl handed Deuce some change and said:

"Son, while you're at the store, would you bring back some Spearmint gum for me?"

When Deuce nodded, Earl gently propelled both girl and boy toward the door.

The shy boy strolled in silence down the sidewalk, trying to think of something to say. As hard as he tried, nothing came to his mind. With every step he took, Deuce felt more embarrassed.

Maria broke the silence. "What happened to the old man who was with you yesterday?"

Deuce had to cough before speaking. "He came down here to make a phone call, then never returned."

"When?" Maria asked.

"Yesterday afternoon."

After ordering a strawberry soda at the soda fountain, Deuce nervously practiced the vertical-shuffle. Maria continued to ask questions, mostly about the cards, getting only brief answers.

Deuce found, that by taking only the top and bottom cards with his right hand as he split the deck, he could move the top card to the bottom and back to the top of the deck with four vertical-shuffles. And he was thankful for the cards ... it was something to talk about.

12

Perfect Pear

Back at the store, Earl the Whirl wasn't solving his mystery --- where the money was --- as easily.
    Fruitless searches of the backroom alternated with periodic entrances of customers. After selling an expensive pair of black wingtips to a man who'd come in asking for marked-down loafers in the window, Earl returned to the back room. While checking the underside of the cot, he heard:
    "Yoo-hoo!" It was a woman's voice.
    "Yoo-hoo!" repeated. "Anybody home?"
    Coming to his feet, Earl walked toward the beaded curtain.
    "*There you are*!" A white-uniformed woman had pushed the curtain aside to look into the back room.
    Earl made out the outline of a pudgy figure. At the woman's ankles, he could clearly see a ridge of flesh overflowing the rims of her low-heels.
    And *a pear you are*! mused Earl. *A perfect pear*.

The middle-aged lady carried a somewhat normal figure above the waist, but was quite chubby below the beltline.

"I've got a problem," Perfect Pear began.

Earl resisted a grin ... plainly seeing the problem.

"As a nurse, I'm on my feet all day," she complained, "and my feet are always sore."

Half-bowing in a cavalier fashion, Earl waved her toward the row of chairs.

"Madam, please have a seat."

Perfect Pear stared at his formal manner for a moment, then waddled around the counter toward a chair. With each step, her girdle made a coarse, scraping protest.

Centering herself on a chair, Perfect Pear hesitantly propped her backside on its metal arms. She began to gently rock from side to side, gradually easing herself past the metal barriers until she was firmly wedged into the chair.

Impressed with the performance, Earl inquired: "Your size, madam?"

"I wear an *eight*," she emphasized.

Before turning away, Earl studied her feet. Selecting two boxes of white leather tennis shoes --- a size nine and ten --- he stopped off at the counter to procure a pair of thick athletic socks.

Earl seated himself before the woman and removed her worn heels. As he did so, he discovered that her outer toes were curled nearly beneath themselves from the pressure of the overly-tight heels. Tenderly, Earl massaged the tortured toes for a moment ... hoping it would make his suggestion more agreeable.

Perfect Pear gratefully grinned. "Honey...you can stop that in a year."

Earl switched to stroking the soles of her feet. "Madam, may I suggest we place athletic stockings over your hose before fitting the new shoes?"

Her face turned suspicious. "I didn't come here to buy socks."

"They're free," Earl offered, "with the shoes."

Perfect Pear nodded. "Go ahead."

He slipped the thick socks over her hose, deciding to try the size-10 shoes first.

"This is the latest design for nurses," Earl told her. "Built-in cushions massage your feet as you walk."

When the tennis shoes were fitted, Earl stood and offered his hand. "Why don't you test them?"

She firmly gripped his hand and heaved herself to a half-standing position.

"Sassafras!" muttered the crouching woman.

Earl gawked at the chair in mid-air. It was attached to her rump.

"Mister" ---Perfect Pear gave him an annoyed look--- "would you mind taking *your* chair?"

"Of course, madam."

Pivoting in small steps, Perfect Pear revolved around until the chair's legs were aimed at Earl.

He glanced at the store entrance to make sure no one was watching, then gripped two legs.

"Pull!" ordered Perfect Pear.

Not wishing to yank the woman off-balance, Earl pulled lightly as she tugged in her own direction. For a short while, the two of them struggled back-and-forth, then Earl began following her around the store like the caboose of a train.

"Hold up!" she called out. "Let me grab something!"

Earl dutifully followed the chair and Perfect Pear to a shelf where she clutched the wooden frame.

"Now pull!" she told him.

Putting all of his weight into the effort, Earl still could not budge the chair from its place.

"I need to sit down," requested the tiring woman. She was perspiring freely.

As Earl guided the legs of the chair, Perfect Pear eased back into a sitting position. Removing his jacket and tidily hanging it on a chair, Earl was about to sit also when she called to him.

"Come over and hold on again!"

When he did as told, she remained seated and began lunging forward instead of upward. As Perfect Pear huffed, the chair scooched across the carpet ... headed for the front door.

"I'm coming free!" exclaimed the woman.

When they paused again to catch their breaths, Earl gaped at the paunch of her hips protruding through each side of the chair. He saw little evidence of progress.

"I *got a feeling*!" she told him with gusto. "Let's go!"

Starting the train again, they were rounding the double-row of chairs by the front door when Perfect Pear popped.

Walking freely, she promptly told him: "You're right! I can feel the cushions."

"They're top-of-the-line," assured Earl, sitting in a chair to rest.

Perfect Pear paced the length of the store and back. Stopping before Earl, she leaned forward to study her new shoes. Unable to see them, she placed one foot far in front to see around her girth. The woman screwed her face into a question and looked Earl squarely in the face.

"Are you sure these are nursing shoes?"

He smiled broadly. "The latest!"

She went in a small circle. "They're *too comfortable* to be nursing shoes."

"Where do you work?" asked Earl, altering the subject.

"UCSD Medical Center."

"When the other nurses see your shoes," Earl assured her, "they're *all* going to want to know where you got them."

Doing another circle, Perfect Pear said mostly to herself: "I could wear these around home, too."

"What's your favorite color?" Earl inquired.

Perfect Pear gave the man a leery eye.

"You can have a second pair for 10 percent off the regular price," he told her.

"How much is one pair?"

Checking the shoe box, he told her: "Only $44.95."

Perfect Pear winced.

"If you'd like another pair," said Earl, "I'll also give you a second pair of stockings."

She pushed a foot out to study the tennis shoes again.

"This is Christmas," nodded Earl the Whirl encouragingly. "Be good to yourself."

He could tell Perfect Pear was wavering.

"What's your favorite color?" Earl again asked.

She looked up. "Light blue."

"Be right back." Earl rapidly sorted through a shelf and returned with two boxes. Removing a pair of blue-and-white checkered tennis shoes, he held them forth.

She snorted. "I don't like checkers."

Opening the other box, Earl displayed a white pair with blue speed stripes along their length. "You'll look fast in these ... even when you're going slow."

She took the shoes and ran her fingers along the stripes.

"Cash, check, or charge, madam?"

Perfect Pear casually responded: "Seems to me, *you're* the fast-mover."

Earl the Whirl grinned impishly with one side of his mouth.

"Cash," she finally said. "Both pairs---the ones I have on and these." She handed over the blue-striped shoes.

"You want to wear what you have on?" he asked.

Glancing at a chair, Perfect Pear shook her head. "Your chairs are too small."

On the way to the cash register, Earl lagged behind and switched the striped shoes from a size-10 box into a size-8 box.

Joining her at the counter, he took the stiff, uncirculated bills she offered and said: "Don't forget to pick out another pair of athletic stockings."

As she poked through a display rack, Earl made change and placed her shoes in a bag. "Send your friends here," Earl told her. "I'll take good care of them."

"You know," she began in a soft voice, "you're the first shoe salesman who ever cared what I was buying."

Earl bowed his head slightly. "You're most gracious, madam."

She leaned over to reach across the counter, then pinched his cheek. "And thanks for the massage, honey. I'll tell my friends about that, too."

When she was almost out of the store, Perfect Pear swung around to call out:

"Merry Christmas!"

Returning the holiday greeting, Earl the Whirl watched her amble out with conflicting thoughts. He didn't mind being thanked when conning someone ... but her gratitude had been too genuine, the voice too warm. And he knew she'd bought twice the shoes she needed.

On the wall beside the register, his eyes noticed a framed quote. Earl recognized its author and read:

The times are piled high with difficulty.
As our case is anew, we must think anew.
We must disenthrall ourselves.
                              ---A. Lincoln

"Think anew?" questioned Earl out loud. "Disenthrall myself?"

To be enthralled is to be captivated, he thought ... and decided the quote was good advice. The words caused him to recollect a story he'd learned as a schoolboy --- of the time Abraham Lincoln, when a storekeeper, had walked ten miles to refund a penny.

Thinking to run after Perfect Pear and return some of her money, Earl hit the double-00 on the register. He picked up the crisp bills she'd given him. As he rubbed their silkiness between his fingers, Earl changed his mind. The money felt too good.

Selling shoes could be fun, the con man told himself.

13

An Honest Day's Work

Deuce was in love, or so he thought.

The new experience---his uncommon confusion and distraction around Maria, his desire to be with her even though at a loss for words, the sense of belonging she gave him---could not be explained otherwise in the mind of the 12-year-old boy.

Their conversation at the soda fountain continued in bits and pieces as Deuce repeated the card trick. Maria mildly teased him when the desired results were not forthcoming ... which was most of the time.

She also asked if he had a girlfriend ... knowing, of course, that the shy boy couldn't possibly have one. But it was a girl's time-honored way of coming around to the subject.

"Not right now," Deuce had responded with a slight cough.

When ordering a second soda, Maria discovered chocolate mint was their favorite ice cream, confirming to her their mutual destiny.

Both boy and girl sensed by the other's tense, yet eager mood, that it was the first date for either. The sharing of the second soda became a ritual of fleeting glances and softly-spoken exchanges.

As they left the drugstore, the boy felt a strong desire to hold the girl's hand...but could not find the nerve to do it.

Sharing his longing but not his shyness, Maria let her hand swing in the same arc as his until it appeared to accidentally touch him. Before they reached the shoe store, he took the hint and loosely hooked her fingers with his.

Earl the Whirl --- with a tinge of regret --- observed the approaching couple from the window of the shoe store. He noted how the timid posturing of their blossoming courtship sharply contrasted with the elegant style of his own contrived affair.

"I can't stay longer," Maria told Deuce at the door. "Tomorrow, I'll be back to pay for my heels."

Glancing downward, Deuce missed her snap smile.

"Thank you," he said, "for helping pick up."

"Bye." Maria half-raised a hand to flick her fingers. "Thanks for the soda."

She ran a few steps down the sidewalk before slowing to a brisk walk. Pivoting into the store, Deuce returned the cards to Earl and asked:

"How do you talk to a girl?"

At Earl's growing grin, Deuce shrugged and said: "I never know what to say."

"It's quite simple, my boy."

Earl the Whirl raised three fingers. "There are three rules for warming up a lady. Compliment her appearance and clothes. Ask her any question about herself. And repeat her name. Everyone likes to hear their name."

"How do you remember all that?"

"Spell out the word *can*," suggested Earl.

"C-A-N."

"Compliment...ask...name," interpreted Earl.

The boy repeated the words in his mind.

Earl handed Deuce the cash he'd taken in. "While you were gone, I sold some shoes."

The boy thumbed through the bills.

"There's $183," said Earl.

Deuce stopped counting and placed the money in the register, deciding to tally it later. The balance of the afternoon ran hot and cold --- the store alternately having only a few browsers or more customers than Earl and Deuce could handle. The boy now had four wads of cash --- a bulging pack of fives in one sock and tens in other one, plus smaller packs of even larger bills growing in his trouser pockets.

While Earl was tied up with a customer, Deuce slipped behind the beaded curtain. Locating *Les Miserables*, he distributed most of the tens and twenties throughout its pages.

Business became brisk in the late afternoon, and they were still selling shoes past 5:30 when Earl checked the wall clock. He interrupted Deuce with a customer.

"I've got a date of my own tonight, young man. Can you handle it from here?"

Deuce nodded. "Sure."

"I'll be going, then."

Earl recovered the briefcase of jewelry and was out the door when Deuce excused himself from his customer. Rushing from the store, he called out:

"Mister!"

Earl the Whirl spun around. The shouted word was something he occasionally heard when a scam hadn't worked as well as it should. Relax, he told himself. You haven't done anything ... yet.

Running up, Deuce bent over to remove four fives from his sock and gave them to the man. "This is for helping today," he explained.

So that's where the kid keeps the money, thought Earl. He contemplated the fives in his palm. They were part of the uncirculated bills he'd received from Perfect Pear. Earl's eyes focused on the sad expression of the Civil War President on the face of the bills.

Honest Abe, silently mused Earl the Whirl.

Frowning, he offered the cash back to the boy as if it was tainted.

"It's yours," insisted Deuce, putting his hands in his pockets.

Earl the Whirl shook his head in the negative, trying to remember the last time he'd come by a *working* dollar. It was a matter of pride to him that he'd never had to "labor" for a living since leaving home. The suggestion now that he had done so made him uneasy. And taking money too early from a mark was another bad habit to start.

Deuce spoke in an encouraging tone. "You coming back tomorrow?"

Earl's expression was meant to raise a doubt in the boy's mind.

"You handled those punks real well," Deuce grinned appreciatively. "And you're teaching me how to sell better, too."

Earl eyed the crisp fives in his hand, considering whether to keep them anyway ... for luck.

"Mister," the boy genuinely appealed, "until Mr Weinstein gets back, I *need* your help."

Earl had heard these words before also. They usually came from a mark. It was a cue that the mark was ready for business. Pursing his lips, the con man scrunched up his face.

"I must return to Chicago soon," Earl said with a difficult smile. "I don't need this money. If you'll take it back, I'll come tomorrow."

"Great!" exclaimed the boy, accepting the fives.

The con man watched Deuce race back to his customer in the store, then spoke to himself in an undertone.

"Don't get any ideas, Mr Lincoln!"

14

One...Maybe Two

As the day ended, the Monterey glided gracefully along at a steady clip through the gently slapping waves. After carrying dry goods in the Sacramento River Delta for 65 years, the remodeled sternwheeler now packaged evening cruises along the balmy waters of San Diego Bay.

Its lower deck was a restaurant. A night club offered live entertainment on the middle deck, with a promenade deck above where Earl and Tanya now strolled after dinner.

When the Monterey passed under the Coronado Bridge, Earl leaned against a handrail and craned his head to take in the great arc. Tanya, her back to his chest, also gazed skyward.

In the evening light, the massive pillars supporting the bridge had taken on a bluish cast. Far above where the pillars ended, the span of the bridge appeared as a curving black void that blocked out the stars.

Earl softly kneaded Tanya's shoulders with his hands while nuzzling her hair, encouraging the woman to squirm even closer.

"San Francisco has the Golden Gate," she observed, "and San Diego has the---"

Tanya searched for words to describe the graceful arch whose western half angled to the north as it descended to land again.

"---the Coronado Curve," offered Earl.

The air being cool, Tanya reached up to draw his arms down and around her.

This is the finest, Earl told himself. The finest I'll ever fleece.

At dinner, Tanya had revealed she was extending her visit in San Diego. The melodic strains of "White Christmas" carried over the splash of the paddlewheel, indicating the band was starting on the deck below.

"Sweet lady," whispered Earl into her ear, "I have a confession to make."

Tanya turned her head enough to catch his eye.

"I'm afraid" ---he lightly brushed her temple with his lips--- "that I'm falling in love."

She came around, within his arms, until they were face-to-face. The woman studied him, her soft eyes becoming intent. Earl sensed what they said, but knew to remain silent ... if he was to learn what this woman's potential was.

She drew apart from Earl, her eyes still fixed to his.

He gathered up her hands as she moved away.

Tanya barely shook her head ... as if in disbelief.

At this reaction, the con man suspected he'd moved too fast. He debated how to backtrack.

"Earl." She said it gently, in a pleading manner.

Pulling her to him, he felt no resistance. They came together and tasted of each other's lips.

Earl broke the embrace to more fully fold the woman in his arms, dotting her face with feather-light kisses.

"I love you, too," she murmured.

After a moment, Earl spoke. "I would dance with you."

From long experience, he knew few things caused a woman's fondness to grow quicker than the ancient rite of dance.

It was some time before they returned to the promenade deck. Tanya had danced until sore feet forced her to remove her heels. After ordering drinks, they silently admired the lights of the bay. Earl loosened his tie, giving his voice a reflective tone.

"Tanya, my dear ... have you ever been in business?"

She gayly laughed. "Goodness, no!"

"I stay active in business because I enjoy it," he told her. "It also can be quite rewarding."

The con man awaited her response; and, when there was none, he continued.

"However, since we met --- to tell the truth --- I'd prefer spending my time with you rather than working."

Tanya smiled through beaming eyes.

"Nevertheless," Earl went on, "I consider it wise to devote at least part of my time doing what I know best ... and that's the retail shoe trade."

When he raised a hand to run a finger along her cheekbone, she kissed the caressing hand.

"Tanya, would you be interested in working with me ... part-time? With your personality, you'd make a fabulous saleslady."

Her eyes opened wide. "I've never worked a day in my life!" Seeing his immediate disappointment, she added: "It might be fun though."

"If you became a partner with me" ---Earl squeezed her hand--- "we could be together more."

Tanya cautiously asked: "What would it involve?"

"Whatever you felt comfortable doing," he told her. "As a matter of fact, in two weeks, I conclude the purchase of a new shoestore in Hillcrest. I'm seeing my banker to arrange a small loan on it tomorrow. We could redecorate the store together, have fun planning a grand opening ... and, like I said, you'd be a great saleslady."

"Where's Hillcrest?" she inquired, sounding interested.

Taking the bait nicely, Earl thought. "It's an older neighborhood to the north of downtown that's experiencing a revival."

"How would you manage two stores?"

Earl paused. "The store where we met belongs to my uncle. He's been ill, and I'm helping out there."

"Who's the boy?"

"Deuce is a fine young man who was helping my uncle when I arrived in San Diego. My uncle trusts him completely. I plan to use Deuce also" --- Earl winked--- "so I don't have to work too many afternoons."

"I might enjoy decorating your new store," Tanya smiled, "but I'm too shy to be a saleslady."

This is a breeze, Earl thought to himself. Don't reel in too fast ... play out some line.

"Selling is more fun than anything else," he told her. "The rest is boring."

She lightly laughed. "I'll stick to the boring parts."

Earl furrowed his brow, giving the appearance of considering a difficult question.

"Tanya, if you're serious about working with me, you could also become a financial partner. I'd let you match my investment."

Earl paused again, permitting the idea to grow.

"It's not necessary to exactly match my investment," he told her. "You could invest whatever amount is convenient ... and we'd still be partners."

Tanya looked directly at him. "How large is your loan?"

Earl the Whirl made a slight smile. The mark was nearly hooked, and he considered how much the woman might be good for.

"The loan is for $22,000," he said.

"Half of that" ---she spoke as if to herself--- "would be $11,000."

Earl set the hook. "Tanya ... if you come in with me, I wouldn't want you to risk your money. Whatever income you're earning on it now, I'd insist on prepaying you a year's interest in the same amount."

Tanya's face brightened. "You would?"

"Absolutely! I wouldn't have it any other way."

Tanya gave him a brief kiss.

"What are your funds earning right now?" he inquired.

She dropped her chin to think. "At the moment, the only available cash I have is a three-year CD that just started last week. It yields 10 percent."

"That's nearly the same rate I was planning to pay my bank," commented Earl. "I'd much prefer to give you the 10 percent than to my bank."

"Why?"

"It would be *smart* business," stated Earl. "It would keep the interest in the family ... so to speak."

Brilliant business, he thought, already composing his *emergency goodbye* note---a precaution learned the hard way after serving his first four-year sentence. Another flim-flam artist had explained: "It's important for the mark to believe you're coming back ... at least long enough for you to get out of the state.

"Earl." Her tone became serious. "Tell me, if I became your partner, how many afternoons a week would you be working?"

Cocking his head to one side, the con man delayed his reply. A respectful smile played on his lips, then broadened.

"You drive a hard bargain, Tanya Toogood."

"Tell me," she insisted.

"One ... maybe two."

Considering his reply only a moment, Tanya asked a more important question. "And...how many nights a week will we go dancing?"

Unlike the first question, this one made Earl stop to think. Dancing with this woman was divine. She anticipated his lead as if she had ESP, and Tanya was the rare woman who did not hang on his shoulder. He took a great deal of pleasure in dancing with her, and he would miss that. His answer came almost reluctantly.

"One ... maybe two."

The woman's face broke into a wide smile. "I'll call my savings and loan in Palm Springs tomorrow to transfer $11,000 to their San Diego branch."

"And I'll give you $1,100 in prepaid interest tomorrow." Earl the Whirl sat taller and extended a hand. "It's a deal."

"I'd rather kiss," she told him.

Having primed and hooked his mark to perfection, Earl eagerly met her anxious lips.

They began to tenderly brush their cheeks together, and Earl felt an instant of regret. In the past, it sometimes bothered him to leave a mark at the height of her passion. And like an actor, at times, he entered into his role ... as Earl knew he was doing this time. While trying to understand his conflicting feelings, his eyes caught the full moon rising over Point Loma. It stood like an icy beacon over the darkened land mass, and he felt a nervous chill at the prospect of the next day.

He kissed Tanya and suggested: "Let's go below and get warm again."

Later when the Monterey docked, Earl escorted Tanya directly to her hotel, explaining he had to rise early the next morning to re-arrange the terms of his escrow for the purchase of the shoe store.

At her suite, Earl permitted himself to be invited inside for a drink .... but he devoted more attention to Trixie than to the dog's mistress. Trixie, remembering the treats of the day before, swiftly cleaned the biscuits from his cuffs. Earl left shortly after finishing the drink and arranging to meet with Tanya the next morning at 11 to exchange checks.

Earl the Whirl had tested both techniques ... finding the "gentleman" approach was far more dependable. It tended to give the mark something to think about besides her money.

❄ **Part Three** ❄

The Day

Before

Christmas

Characters & *Props* for Part Three

15   Earl the Whirl - *briefcase w/ jewelry box*
            Deuce - *large book, play money*
            Pawnbroker
            Gretchen

16   Earl the Whirl - *envelope cash*
            Tanya - *shower cap*
            Trixie
            1st Beautician(Agnes)
            2nd Beautician
            Hotel Clerk

17   Maria's Mother
            Maria - *red heels*
            Deuce - *shoe boxes*
            Spike - *chair*
            Cruz
            Joe

18   Earl the Whirl - *stuffed envelope*
            Deuce - *play money*
            Maria
            Policeman

19   Deuce
            Maria - *mistletoe*
            Trixie
            Tanya - *shopping bag*
            Earl the Whirl
            An Elderly Man - *chair*

15

It Looks Like A Ruby

After Earl the Whirl checked out of the Hudson House, he went to the Greyhound bus station where he placed his flightbag in a locker.

Earl arrived in front of the shoe store shortly before 10 a.m. Deuce was nowhere in sight.

Pacing impatiently, the con man switched his briefcase from hand to hand. A bus passed by and Earl heard someone yell: "Hi!"

He followed the bus with his eyes and saw a boy holding onto the back of it. The bus slowed, and Deuce jumped off ... expertly hitting the street on the run.

As Deuce ran back toward the store, Earl checked the time and noticed that the ruby ring was still on his finger. Moving within the store's doorway, he took the ring off and placed it in the briefcase.

"Hi!" exclaimed the boy again.

"Good morning, Deuce." The con man held a troubled expression.

"Is something wrong?" asked the boy.

"Let's go inside and I'll tell you."

Earl walked to the back of the store and sat down with a sigh. His manner reminded Deuce of the storeowner two days earlier. The con man placed the briefcase on the chair between them.

"I received a call from Chicago last night," he began. "I have to return there immediately." Earl leaned toward Deuce and closely scrutinized him. "Young man, can I trust you?"

The boy nodded.

"If I could leave this jewelry with you" ---Earl placed a hand on the briefcase--- "to give to my uncle, it'd save me the expense of returning to San Diego again."

Earl unsnapped the briefcase and removed the lacquered box. Seeing the boy's eyes fix on the inlaid peacock lid, Earl raised it. The ruby ring glittered atop the other jewels.

"Deuce, I can't leave this in San Diego unless you replace my performance bond."

The boy looked up bewildered. "What's a performance bond?"

Earl made a show of checking his watch. "My bu--- uh ---plane leaves in an hour."

Hesitating, the con man gave Deuce a look as if he was debating what to do ... then cast the hook.

"A performance bond guarantees a person will perform a task. To guarantee I'd deliver this jewelry to my uncle, I was required to deposit $1,100 with a court of law in Chicago."

Deuce listened intently as Earl continued.

"Before I can leave this briefcase here, you'd have to deposit the same amount of money with me ... to guarantee *you* would give it to my uncle."

"Do I get the money back?" said Deuce.

Of course." Earl frowned at the question. "I'll give your receipt for the jewelry to the court in Chicago, and they'll return my money. Then I'll send your money back to you."

Deuce chewed at his lip, wondering what Mr Weinstein would want him to do. He stared into the rich glow of the red gem, knowing it would impress Maria. Deuce even dared to think of asking the storeowner for the ring. Mr Weinstein was a generous man, and there was plenty of other jewelry.

Earl went on. "The ruby ring alone is worth several times $1,100. Why don't we visit the pawnshop down the block and get an appraisal of it?"

When Deuce made no objection, the con man put the ring in his pocket and told the boy: "Lock up the store."

As they walked to the pawnshop, Earl said: "It's best if only you and I know what's within this briefcase. That's why I took the ring out."

Inside the shop, Earl handed the ring to the baldheaded pawnbroker. "Sir, could you appraise this ruby for us?"

The pawnbroker yelled over his shoulder: "Gretchen! Bring me my eyepiece."

A thin woman, dusting a guitar case, replied in a reedy voice. "It's under the elephant!"

Finding his eyepiece under an ebony elephant, the pawnbroker examined the ring.

"This is aluminum oxide," he announced in a deadpan voice.

Earl the Whirl's mouth dropped open.

The bald man laughed at his small joke.

"Those are the *natural* elements of a ruby," he explained. "Now, let's find out if it's synthetic or genuine."

Pulling a small microscope from under the counter, he viewed the ring from three different angles and impressively murmured: "No bubbles ... some streaks, though. It's real."

"What's its value?" Earl impatiently asked.

The pawnshop was empty of customers, and its owner was in no hurry to give free advice. He'd viewed the gem's optical axis from several angles.

"Are you interested in a loan?" asked the pawnbroker. "Or selling it? I can give you more if you're selling it."

"We want a loan appraisal," repeated Earl, regretting that he hadn't taken the time to check out the pawnshop in advance.

Thinking to be on the safe side, Deuce said: "We *might* sell it."

"Gentlemen" ---the bald man set the ring back on the counter and folded his arms together--- "make up your minds."

"Give us both figures!" demanded Earl in an annoyed tone. He looked to his watch. It was past 10:30.

The pawnbroker viewed the ring under the microscope one more time and spoke first to the con man. "If you want a loan, I'd give you $1,500." Turning to the boy, he added: "If you'll sell it, I'll give you $2,000."

"Thank you, sir!" responded Earl, snatching the ring off the microscope plate and putting it on his finger.

As the con man hurried out of the pawnshop, the pawnbroker rushed after him.

"I'll give you $2,500 to buy the ring!" called out the pawnbroker from his door.

"It's not for sale!" barked Earl.

After a brief pause, the pawnbroker yelled: "Three-thousand!"

Ignoring the offer, the con man forced a smile before posing a question of Deuce.

"You feel better about putting up the $1,100 now?"

Deuce nibbled at his lip some more.

"Doesn't the store have $1,100?" asked Earl.

Afraid to make a decision, Deuce parried: "I don't know."

Earl glanced at his watch again. Tanya would be waiting for him in 17 minutes.

"Tell you what, Deuce. If you have a $1,000, I'll trust you for that."

The boy pointed toward the back of the store. "Let me check."

Following Deuce as far as the counter, Earl waited as the boy went through the curtain. Deuce promptly returned with a book.

He placed *Les Miserables* on the countertop and began removing cash from its pages. Deuce counted the bills into stacks of $100 as he took them from the book.

"There's $1,000," said the boy.

Earl hastily wrote out a receipt for the jewelry and had Deuce sign it. The con man then scooped up the cash and again checked his watch.

"Geez!" he exclaimed. "I may miss my plane!"

Earl pushed the briefcase across the counter to Deuce. "Hide this in back...and I advise you to tell no one you have it."

With that, the con man pivoted and rushed toward the door, calling over his shoulder: "Good luck, kid!"

"You forgot something!" shouted Deuce, running after him.

Earl paused at the store entrance.

The boy pointed to the con man's hand. "The ruby ring," said Deuce. "You forgot to put it back in the box."

Earl the Whirl debated a moment whether to keep going ... or give up the ring. Thinking of the $11,000 waiting for him in less than 12 minutes, he decided to return for the ring later.

"That's right," grinned Earl, removing the ring from his finger and handing it over. "We forgot."

Deuce jutted his chin out and spoke earnestly. "Thanks for everything."

The boy's sincerity made Earl pause. He reached over to tousle Deuce"s curly blond hair. "Next time I'm in town, I'll show you another card trick."

"Next time," repeated the boy.

Earl the Whirl squeezed the boy's shoulder before hurrying down the sidewalk.

Deuce held the ring in the sunlight, looking for the streaks mentioned by the pawnbroker. In the bright light, he couldn't see them but he did note a greenish cast to the stone. Moving back within the store and out of the sunlight, Deuce no longer saw the green color and tried the ring on his fingers.

He found it was too small, but that was fine. The boy intended to give the ring to Maria ... if Mr Weinstein would first give it to him.

Earl silently cursed his mistake as he rounded the corner. Why didn't you return the ring to the jewelry box along the sidewalk? Then you could have retrieved it in the shoe store. You're getting rusty, he warned himself. Remembering the $1,000 was a $100 short of the amount he'd promised to give Tanya, Earl removed cash from his wallet to make up the difference.

In the pawnshop, Gretchen thought to ask her husband why he'd become so excited over the ruby ring.

"It wasn't a ruby," he responded.

"What was it?"

"An alexandrite."

"Never heard of that," commented Gretchen.

"They're rare ... extremely rare. The gem was first discovered in Russia," the pawnbroker explained, "when the second Alexander became czar. So, it was named in his honor."

"How do you know that's what it was?"

"Under the microscope, I viewed it from three different directions. The color changed from red to orange-yellow to emerald green. Only an alexandrite does that."

The pawnbroker paused.

"And in artificial light, an alexandrite looks like a ruby, but in sunlight it takes on the quality of an emerald. I saw it do that at the door."

"What's it worth?" asked Gretchen.

The pawnbroker pondered the question a moment.

"A stone that large---at one time---may even have belonged to the Romanovs. I'd say it's worth 20 to 30 times the finest ruby of equal size."

"Do you think the man knew that?"

"I doubt it," said the pawnbroker. "If he had, he wouldn't have brought it in here."

16

"See You At Noon"

At Suite 322, Earl the Whirl hesitated as he started to knock on the door. Feeling short of breath, he inhaled deeply to calm himself before raising his hand again. He lightly tapped. Too lightly, he decided when no response came. Earl rapped a bit harder. Over Trixie's yipping, he faintly heard a voice.

"Who's there?"

"Me ... Earl."

The door came half-open and Trixie jumped out.

Tanya was wrapped in a pink bathrobe and, obviously, just out of a shower. Over her hair she still wore a wet shower cap. She looked at him in mild surprise.

"I didn't expect you so soon."

Earl dropped his gaze to Trixie, whose paws were busy working his cuffs in search of snacks. Fumbling in his jacket, the con man withdrew a thick envelope and offered it.

"Your interest, my dear. One full year, in advance."

Tanya peeked inside the flap and looked up. "I thought you would give me a check."

Earl shrugged casually. "I had the cash on me."

"I'm afraid I don't have my check yet," said Tanya, stuffing Earl's envelope in a pocket of her robe. "Mr Hashagen, the local manager of my savings and loan, called to say there'd be an hour's delay in delivering it. He said they were swamped with customers ... this being Christmas Eve."

Staring dumbly at the tip of the envelope showing from her pocket, the con man briefly considered reaching over to retrieve it.

"Earl, why don't we move our lunch date to twelve ... right after my check arrives?"

"Well..." He felt out of breath again. This isn't supposed to be happening, Earl told himself, and he thought to tell the same to the woman. Instead, he weakly smiled.

"Good!" declared Tanya. "I knew you'd agree. After Mr Hashagen called, I made a hairdresser appointment for 11:15."

"Where's your hairdresser?" Earl blurted out.

Registering some surprise at his question, Tanya replied: "They told me just around the block."

Tanya puckered her lips and kissed him. "See you at noon, okay?"

"Sure," he vacantly replied.

Gathering up Trixie, she closed the door.

Earl returned to the lobby and purchased a newspaper before sitting in a stuffed chair. When he was midway through the sports section, Tanya came through the lobby, dressed in white, her hair hidden by a red turban. Earl wondered why she carried a bulging shopping bag.

He stood as Tanya hesitated at the hotel's entrance to scan the block. When she turned right, Earl briskly strode to the sidewalk and saw her round a corner.

When the con man turned the same corner, the red turban was nowhere in sight. No longer concerned with concealing himself, Earl lurched forward, examining the interior of each passing storefront. Near the end of the short block, it became evident no beauty salon fronted the sidewalk on either side of the street.

Reversing his direction, Earl slipped inside the few foyers he'd rushed by and found "Carnie's Coiffeurs" within the second one. Cautiously, he peered within the salon.

Tanya stood, her back to him, engaged in conversation with a beautician. Edging out of the foyer, Earl jaywalked through traffic to a coffee shop directly across the street.

At a window booth, he ordered a cinnamon roll with coffee ... and checked his watch. It read 11:28. After finishing the sports section, Earl ordered a second coffee upon inquiring if it was free. He took small measured bites from the roll to make it last as long as possible.

The caffeine of the coffee only made him more jumpy. When he finished the newspaper, Earl switched his attention to the foyer across the street. Where should I play the $11,000? he pondered. Either Reno or Las Vegas, he decided. Earl could make out a slight reflection of himself in the glass of the window. He looked tired.

"This is getting to be too much for you," he softly told his image. "You've got to find another line. And you asked for too little money, considering how quickly she came around. She's probably worth $500,000 ... maybe a million."

Though his gaze was still directed across the street, the foyer no longer focused in his eyes. Instead, he envisioned the height of $500,000 ... stacked in twenties. He decided it had to be at least eight feet high.

"You fool --- you crazy fool!" Earl spoke in a near-normal voice to his reflection on the glass.

"You could have it all! You could marry her and have it all. And you're running away. Away from five-hundred grand!" For a moment, Earl imagined what life would be like with no more cons ... no more running ... no more hard time ... no more cold nights.

It was the first time he'd seriously considered being a husband and the first time he hadn't cringed at the possibility. "I like Tanya," he told himself. "I could even learn to love her."

Earl watched the people rushing by his window, hurrying to complete their Christmas shopping. Tonight, he thought, they'll be with friends and family.

"I've got it," Earl said quietly to himself. "I could tell Tanya that the storeowner in Hillcrest cancelled the escrow. And I'll keep working at the store with the kid. It's good pocket money ... like a pension." Earl paused, wondering why he was having such ideas. "Maybe, you love her already," he suggested to himself.

The con man nodded to confirm his thought, then checked his watch. It read 11:48.

"I'll tell her right now!" Earl exclaimed.

He threw money for the bill on the table and rushed out. At the beauty parlor, Earl halted just inside the door. Four chairs lined each side of the small shop and were occupied by smock-covered customers, their faces looking like they'd been smeared by a white paint-roller.

The nearest beautician excused herself from a customer and asked Earl: "Do you have an appointment?"

He looked at her wide-eyed.

She continued in a scolding manner. "We work by appointment and---"

Earl loudly interrupted. "I'm looking for a lady in white."

"Which one?" The beautician gave him a smirky smile, jerking her chin over her shoulder at the eight white-smocked customers.

The painted faces had turned to glare at the noisy intruder. Earl stared back, not recognizing anything familiar behind the paint. He offered:

"She had a red turban."

Another beautician spoke up. "Agnes, he's talking about the lady who came in a half-hour ago."

"Oh, yes," Agnes recalled. "We had no appointment for her, and couldn't fit her in."

Earl stumbled out of the parlor. No appointment, he repeated in his mind. How could that be? Tanya said she *had* one. It occurred to him the appointment must have been at some other beauty shop, and Earl trooped back into Carnie's Coiffeurs to ask:

"Is there another beauty parlor around here?"

Agnes shook her head. "I'm new here, mister." The other beautician told him: "Take a left at the end of the block, then look for Freda's Fancy."

Earl found the second beauty shop, but none of the hooded customers wore white slacks and no one had seen a red turban.

He checked his watch again. It read 11:59.

Back at the U.S. Grant, there was no response to Earl's knocking at Suite 322. When not even the yipping of Trixie came after a minute, Earl played a hunch.

At the hotel check-in desk, he butted in front of two other persons and addressed the clerk.

"Excuse me! I have an emergency. Is Tanya Toogood still registered in Suite 322?"

The clerk checked his computer and gave a prim reply. "We have no one by that name, sir."

Stricken-faced, the con man gripped the counter.

"She did me," he whispered disbelievingly to himself. "She *actually* did me."

"Sir," said the clerk, "if you'll step aside, I have other customers."

Wandering out of the hotel, Earl stood on the sidewalk, letting the vacuum in his mind gradually fill. The flexing of the finely-muscled legs ... the hundred-dollar bill ... the press of her dancing ... the shifting of the luncheon date ... the bulging shopping bag ... *the accent*.

It was all a game, Earl decided, and *I* was the mark.

I should have known by the accent, he kept repeating. I should have known by the accent.

In the community of con artists, only a few fleeced their own. Since word of such dealings passed swiftly, the successful tricksters were usually from out of the country.

A half-block from the U.S. Grant, Earl the Whirl rested on a bus bench. He closed his eyes to knead his brow. When he re-opened his eyes, they focused on the light band of skin circling his ring finger where the red jewel had been.

17

"Don't Like Being Jabbed"

Maria removed the red heels from her feet and handed them to her mother, who massaged their leather doubtfully.

"Honey, are you sure this is what you want for Christmas?"

Maria eagerly nodded. "I can wear them with most anything."

Handing the heels back to Maria, the mother opened her purse. "How much did you say they were?"

"Twenty-nine---" began Maria.

Deuce cut in. "Nineteen dollars."

The mother looked to Deuce.

"She helped me clean up yesterday," he explained.

Maria's mother gave the money to Deuce, then spoke to her daughter. "I'm doing some more shopping. Do you want to come with me?"

"Not really," the girl replied.

"Then, we'll meet here in two hours."

"Thanks, Mom."

After depositing the money in the register, Deuce came back to Maria, who was modeling her new heels before a full-length mirror. Standing behind her, he spoke the four words he'd been rehearsing since he'd last seen her.

"Your hair is pretty."

With a quick movement of her head, Maria gaped at the boy. And for a moment, Deuce had the dread feeling he'd said something terribly wrong.

"Uh ... you ... you like my hair?" stammered the girl. Her startled expression changed to a shy smile.

Deuce nodded. And encouraged, he asked his second question.

"What's your middle name?"

Maria giggled. "You don't even know my last name yet."

Deuce shuffled his feet and laughed at himself. "What's your whole name?"

"Maria Theresa Carillo."

"I like Theresa," he promptly said.

The girl smiled. "Mom uses it when she's mad at me."

"Maria sounds nice, too," said Deuce, thinking he'd completed the code given him by Earl ... and it was working great. He decided to start over again.

"The red heels look good on you."

She examined herself in the mirror again and nodded: "I like being taller."

With the heels on, she could nearly look the boy in the eye. He remembered the question Earl had asked of the pink lady.

"When are you going to wear them?"

Maria gave it some thought. "To the movies."

"What movie did you see yesterday?" Deuce asked.

"Star Wars 7."

"Did you like it?"

"Super," she replied.

The boy, thoroughly pleased with himself, could think of a multitude of compliments and questions. Feeling the ring in his pocket, he pulled it out and pretended to study it.

"Wow!" exclaimed Maria, coming closer to examine the ring. "What is it?"

"A ruby." Deuce offered it to her. "See if it fits you."

She tried to fit it, but the ring was too loose on her slender fingers.

The boy dipped his head and lowered his voice. "Maria, put it on your thumb."

"Where's the bossman?" called out the white punk. Spike was followed into the store by Joe and Cruz.

"What do you want?" retorted Deuce, putting anger in his tone.

"What do yooo-uuu want?" repeated Spike mockingly. He paused to look at the shoeshine boy and Maria. "We want to be paid ... for our *protection*."

Deuce met the punk's glare with his own. "I don't have any money."

"You got shoes," nodded Spike with a snicker. Strolling to a shelf, he pulled off a box and tossed it to Deuce.

"Whadda you think? Do they fit me?"

Studying Spike's scuffed loafers, Deuce looked at the size on the box. "They're probably too small."

"Well, how 'bout a pair that fits!" he demanded. Grinning at his buddies, Spike plopped down in a chair.

Deuce cast a brief look at Maria. She'd remained beside him, and he whispered: "Stay where you are."

As Deuce searched for another pair of loafers, Joe and Cruz ambled toward the rear of the store and began inspecting display items on the counter.

When Deuce returned to Spike with shoes, Cruz eased around the counter and slipped behind the beaded curtain. As his eyes adjusted to the dark, he moved into the shadows ... tripping over an object on the floor. Cruz gave the backroom a quick once-over, finding nothing worth taking. Heading back to the curtain, he recognized the briefcase over which he'd stumbled and gave it a kick.

When something clattered inside the briefcase, Cruz crouched to open it and removed the lacquered box. After raising the peacock lid, he made a smacking sound with his lips and tucked the box under his shirt.

Cruz paused at the edge of the curtain; and, seeing Deuce still occupied, came through the beads. He sauntered to a position behind Deuce. Giving a thumbs-up to Spike, Cruz then moved toward the store's entrance.

"These stink!" snapped Spike, kicking off the shoes that Deuce had brought him. He shoved his loafers back on and came to his feet. Jabbing an index finger into Deuce's chest, he spit out:

"We'll be back, Short-Stuff. Have our mon---"

Spike stared at his finger, which Deuce had enveloped in an iron grip.

"Leggo, you twerp!" squawked Spike, trying to yank it away. When he couldn't, the white youth swung his free hand.

Stepping inside the punch, Deuce caught Spike's flying wrist. With both of the punk's hands immobilized, Deuce started to bend the index finger backwards.

"Yeeoowww!" squealed Spike, forced back into his chair again.

Joe came forward.

"Back off!" growled Deuce, "or I'll break his finger."

"Get away from me, Joe!" yelled Spike. "Do what he says."

Deuce's voice came low and steady. "Now ... tell your funny-looking friends to get out of my store."

"*Okay ... okay,*" Spike pleaded. "Ease up, man. I was *only* kidding."

"Out!" repeated Deuce, putting more pressure on the finger.

"You heard him!" Spike shouted at the two other punks. "GET OUT!"

They backed toward the door.

"Hey, man," whined Spike in a low voice the others couldn't hear. "You're hurting me."

"I don't like being jabbed," Deuce stated coldly.

Spike lowered his voice even more. "I'm sorry, man. Okay?"

Checking the entrance of the store where Cruz and Joe waited, Deuce released the white youth's hands.

Spike remained in the chair, massaging his finger. ""You're fast, dude," he said. "Maybe, I can use you."

Deuce jerked his head toward the street. "Out of my store."

At the door, Spike pointed his sore finger at Deuce. "Watch yourself, Short-stuff."

When the trio was out of sight, Maria broke the silence. "Where'd you learn to do that?"

Deuce picked up the box of loafers, then looked to Maria. "What?"

"Grabbing his hands like that."

"From a book."

She squinted. "A book?"

The boy nodded.

"Which one?"

"*Of Mice and Men.*"

It drew a blank on Maria's face.

"Well, I didn't actually learn it from a book," Deuce shrugged. "Just the idea."

She stared in awe. "Do you read many books?"

Deuce wondered whether she'd laugh at him if he told the truth ... that he read two to three books a week.

He nodded. "When I have time."

18

Copasetic!

Earl the Whirl had bought another newspaper and envelope, plus a cheap scissors. In a greasy diner, while nursing a bowl of soup, he fished through his pockets to count his money. It totaled $87.31.

Taking a $20 bill from his wallet, the con man began cutting the newspaper to match the twenty in size. After 15 minutes, he stuffed the results in the new envelope, placing the $20 bill so it would show as he raised the flap.

At the shoe store, Earl the Whirl saw Deuce and Maria before they spotted him. He hung back at the entrance, taking in the sweet simplicity of the young couple ... coveting the glow of their enchantment.

The con man had little stomach for what he was about to do, and he paused to let his twinge of conscience pass.

The money Tanya took was not the kid's money, Earl told himself. It belonged to the old man who'd collapsed in the phone booth ... and he certainly doesn't need it anymore. So what're you worried about? he prodded his conscience. Get the ruby and get out.

While Earl debated what to do at the door, the boy and girl stood at opposite sides of the back counter, leaning toward each other. Maria toyed with the ring, rotating it round her thumb. From his position, the con man could not distinguish the object of their attention.

Noticing Earl, Deuce called out: "Miss your plane?"

The con man absently shook his head and uttered. "She's gone."

"Who's gone?" asked the boy, walking to the front of the store.

"Tanya," mumbled Earl.

"The pink lady?"

Earl nodded. Moving just inside the store, the con man pulled out a thick envelope.

"Deuce, I have to return the $1,000 to you."

Earl opened the flap of the envelope part way to flash the face of a $20 bill.

The boy looked from the twenty to the man. "I thought---"

"I can't take it," interrupted Earl. "It's not your money to give me. I've decided it'd be better for me to hold the ruby ring as your bond."

Deuce glanced to Maria, who had followed along behind him. The girl waited to be asked for the ring's return, but Deuce---more reluctant to part with it than even Maria---could only stare at the gem on her finger.

Spotting the ring, Earl assumed it had been given to Maria and he realized with a frown that he would be taking it from the girl also, What a bum I am, Earl told himself.

Yet, when Maria offered the ring, he quickly took it. Earl handed the fat envelope to Deuce. Then---from the corner of his eye---the con man became aware of another person slightly behind him.

Pivoting, Earl saw black-on-black and froze.

The black gabardine worn by the broad-chested man blended with his coal-colored skin. He towered over the con man, whose attention riveted on a silver badge over the man's heart. And in the groves of the rectangular badge, Earl visualized the bars of a cell.

"Does this belong to you?" asked the black policeman. He held out the lacquered box with the peacock lid.

Earl was too startled to speak.

The officer continued. "Some hoods in the back of my car say it came from this store."

Seeing the patrol car through a window, Earl accepted the box and opened it. The jewelry was still within.

The cop jerked a thumb at his car. "The hoods tried to pawn that stuff up the street, but the pawnbroker called us, thinking it might be stolen. When the hoods found out the jewelry was fake, they said it came from here."

Earl the Whirl sighed heavily. He locked eyes with Deuce a long moment before handing the lacquered box to him. Earl spoke in a faltering voice.

"The boy here is supposed to be holding it for someone."

Studying Earl a moment, the officer addressed Deuce. "Is that right, son?"

Deuce nodded agreement.

The officer observed the boy a moment, then came back to Earl. "Since the jewelry's worthless, do either of you mind if I take it down to the station as evidence? It'll keep those hoods off the streets for the rest of the day."

Earl the Whirl managed a shaky grin. "That's fine, officer."

After Deuce handed over the box, the police officer paused to examine the con man's features. "Haven't I seen your face somewhere, mister?"

"Uh ... maybe ... I'm active in civic groups downtown," sputtered Earl. "I work with homeless kids, like Deuce here."

Both men looked to Deuce, who took in the pleading expression on the con man's face before speaking.

"That's right," Deuce offered.

"The D.A.'s office will be getting in touch within a few days," said the officer, "if you want to press charges." With that, the policeman turned and stalked out of the store.

When the patrol car had pulled away, Earl the Whirl plopped down in a chair. He turned to Deuce with a wan smile.

"Thanks, kid ... thanks for covering for me."

Leaving an empty chair between them, Deuce also sat and uncertainly fingered the thick envelope in his hands. He was thinking of the monte game with the three punks and now the fake jewelry. Deuce fought an impulse to open the envelope. *For the sake of a bone* ran through his mind ... and the boy recalled the second chance given him by Mr Weinstein. Deuce hesitated ... not wishing to prove the man a dog.

Earl pulled the ring from his pocket and cautiously observed: "I guess this ring's the only valuable piece of jewelry in the lot."

The man waited for a response from Deuce, afraid to look the boy in the eye.

Finally, Earl bowed his head and wracked his brain. How could I come so close to so much ... and now have nothing? He stared down at the ring in his hand, shifting it slightly in the light to better view its warm luster. Then, Earl remembered what he did have.

I have this ruby, he told himself ... and more important, I still have my *freedom*, thanks to the boy.

Earl continued to rotate the gem before his eyes, enjoying the beauty of its radiance. An admiring smile grew on his face ... and faded.

Without fully understanding his action, Earl reached out to place the ring squarely on the empty seat between the boy and himself. The con man continued to gaze at the ring. For all its beauty, he realized the jewel had not brought him happiness. It was only a tool to fool ... a ticket to run ... to chase the impossible.

And I don't want to lose anymore, Earl told himself. He looked up, now willing to meet the eyes of the boy.

"Take the ring, Deuce. And return the envelope to me."

Deuce considered the ring, then the envelope in his hand.

"Look, kid," Earl twisted his face in a grimace. "I'm not who I said I was. The owner of this store had a heart attack in a hotel lobby where I was staying. I walked around till I found this place."

As he continued to talk, the con man looked out the door through which he would soon leave.

"The money you gave me this morning is gone ... the pink lady tricked me out of it. Her hotel told me she's not there anymore." Earl dolefully added: "I saw her leave with her stuff."

Earl the Whirl made the mistake of meeting Deuce's eyes again ... and saw the bitterness of betrayal. Earl didn't know which was worse. The loss of the woman who had charmed him so ... or his guilt for duping this boy who looked up to him and had even protected him.

Picking up the ring, Earl tucked it in a pocket of Deuce's shirt and tried to speak. His throat was dry, and he had to swallow before hoarsely whispering:

"Merry Christmas."

Earl sensed a loss in parting with the one possession he valued most, but he also felt a heavy burden lift from his mind. Though he didn't understand his feelings, they were refreshing, and that surprised him.

It was not like after the huge losses he suffered at the gambling tables. Those losses were embarrassing ... degrading ... a symbol of stupidity. Strangely enough, Earl found his emotions to be the exact opposite. And most of all, he didn't have that terrible sense of emptiness that came when all the chips had finally been lost.

Wishing to be alone with his thoughts, Earl abruptly stood and trudged toward the door.

"Mister!" Deuce called out.

Not wanting to talk further, Earl increased his pace, forcing Deuce to run after him. When he felt a hand on the sleeve of his jacket, Earl paused for the boy.

The con man slowly turned his head; and, instead of the bitterness he'd seen before, Earl now saw excitement. The joy of receiving the ruby, thought Earl.

Deuce held up the $20 bill he'd removed from the thick envelope.

"This is yours," said Deuce.

"That's alright, kid." Earl shook his head.

"It's yours," insisted Deuce, slipping the twenty into a pocket of the man's jacket.

Still holding onto the sleeve, Deuce said: "I learned a lot from you."

Earl had to look away. "I hope not too much."

"I can talk with Maria now," Deuce proudly grinned.

Glancing at Maria in the store, Earl nodded knowingly to Deuce. "I think she likes you, kid. If you want, give the ring to her. Maybe, someday..." His forlorn voice trailed off.

In the awkward silence, Deuce said: "I won't forget you."

Removing his Panama hat, Earl the Whirl reached over to tousle the curly blond hair again. He wondered what it would've been like to have a son like the boy ... and smiled at the thought.

"Copacetic."

Deuce squinted. "What's that mean?"

"You're okay," Earl nodded to the boy. "It means you're first-rate."

He offered his hand to Deuce, who returned a firm grip.

Hesitantly, Earl backed away a few steps.

When Deuce raised a hand in farewell, Earl the Whirl tipped his white Panama hat and turned away.

19

A Piece of Mistletoe

A customer had entered the shoe store following Earl's departure; and, after selling another pair of shoes, Deuce sat down beside Maria before opening his palm.
"He said I could give it to you."
The red gem glowed in his hand.
Maria lifted her eyes to his. "Can we share it ... can it be *our* ring?"
Deuce shrugged with a grin. "Why not?"
The girl moved nearer to him before closing her eyes. A moment later, she pursed her lips for a kiss --- commanding his response.
Deuce stiffened. Though he wished to kiss her, he hesitated.
After five seconds, the girl still resisted the temptation to open her eyes.
To the timid boy, it seemed like five minutes.

Eyes closed, Maria smiled encouragement, making her lips even more attractive to the boy.

Puckering his own lips, Deuce positioned his face directly before hers, then closed his own eyes.

And touched noses.

The yipping of a dog gave them a double-start.

Turning their heads, they saw Trixie pulling excitedly at her leash, prancing from side to side at the store entrance.

"Excuse me," offered Tanya, having seen the supposed kiss.

She carried a bulky shopping bag through the door. Her white outfit was accented by a scarlet sash at the waist and a blue wide-brimmed hat. Trixie's satin bow matched the hat.

"Has Earl" ---she paused out of breath--- "been here in the last hour?"

Deuce cautiously offered: "He left a little while ago."

"Oh, dear!" Tanya brought her hands to her heaving chest. "I missed him again. I hope he isn't unhappy with me."

Untangling her heels from the leash, Tanya set the shopping bag down and sat. "I have to rest a moment."

Deuce exchanged glances with Maria before telling the woman:

"He's gone."

Tanya's head twisted to the boy. "What did you say?"

"He thought *you* disappeared," stated Deuce, adding: "with his money."

"Oh, my goodness!" The woman's hand went from her mouth to her purse, which she patted. "I have his money right here ... ready for him."

"Your hotel told him you'd checked out," said Deuce.

Tanya shook her head in confusion. "I *haven't* checked out."

She looked from boy to girl, both of whom still eyed her with suspicion. The woman spoke as to herself. "I must have registered at the hotel in my maiden name."

Becoming teary-eyed, Tanya realized exactly what they were thinking and tried to explain.

"After a mix-up at the hairdresser, I went directly to my savings and loan to pick up a check for him. Earl was to meet me at noon, and when he didn't arrive by a quarter-after, I stepped out to exchange a Christmas gift at a store across the street from the hotel. I thought he'd wait."

Composing herself, Tanya asked, "Where did he go?"

"I think the airport," Deuce offered. "He had a TWA flight bag."

Tanya stood. "I must find him." She held the dog's leash out to the boy. "Can you watch Trixie for me until I return? Taxi drivers won't stop for me when I have her."

When Deuce accepted the leash, the woman rushed out. He knelt beside the excited poodle and stroked its back until the dog's cries for its mistress lessened.

"Do you think she's telling the truth?" wondered Deuce out loud.

"*Of course*," asserted Maria. "She was crying. And she left her dog."

Deuce continued to pet Trixie, who was now busily sniffing Earl's scent on the strips of newspaper the con man had cut to the shape of a $20 bill. A few strips had dropped to the carpet when Deuce withdrew the real $20 bill and rushed after Earl.

"Cute dog," Maria commented.

Deuce wasn't listening.

"I don't think Earl was headed for the airport," he said, throwing the leash in her direction. "Watch the dog for me."

Running out the door, Deuce heard loud yipping and glanced behind to see the dog bounding after him. He stopped to scoop up the racing dog and missed, but caught her trailing leash.

Trixie, her nose to the sidewalk, raced ahead of the boy. Pausing at redlights long enough to dodge traffic, Deuce let Trixie lead him the seven blocks to the Greyhound station.

Inside the building, Deuce put down the dog, keeping hold of her leash. The poodle scurried up and down aisles ... sniffing at the pants cuffs of everyone it passed.

The boy permitted himself be towed to a ticket window. From there, Trixie headed out of the waiting room and into the garage where buses waited to depart.

A row of three Greyhounds were lined up. As Trixie sniffed around in a small circle, Deuce scanned the windows along the side of the first bus. When he ran down the side of the second bus, pulling Trixie along behind, the dog strained at her leash in protest.

To check the third bus, Deuce had to drag the protesting toy poodle backwards. Yapping even louder than before, Trixie furiously worked her little padded feet in the opposite direction.

When Deuce didn't find Earl's face along the third bus, he realized his mistake and released her leash.

Trixie took off like a rocket, making a beeline for the first bus, which was pulling out of its spot and preparing to enter street traffic. When Deuce caught up, Trixie was jumping into the air to scratch at the glass of the bus door.

The boy pounded on the door to get the driver's attention, but the driver mouthed words Deuce couldn't hear and waved the boy away. Catching Trixie in the air at mid-jump, Deuce tucked her under his arm and ran down the bus to check the windows on the other side.

As they rounded the back of the Greyhound, it belched a black cloud of fumes and started to move out into traffic. Deuce ran with the bus as it entered the street and was halfway up its other side when he caught a glimpse of the white Panama hat.

Coming dangerously close to the moving bus, Deuce jumped up to bang the window.

Earl the Whirl turned a withered brow. Recognizing the frantically waving boy and thinking Deuce had come to give another goodbye, Earl wanly waved his own hand.

Gaining speed, the bus outdistanced the running boy. At the next intersection when the bus paused to turn, Deuce caught up enough to grab the grill over its rear. With an arm hooked over the top of the grill and his feet on the bumper, he struggled to tuck Trixie inside his shirt.

When the bus driver halted for a red light, the boy hopped off and banged again below Earl's window. This time Deuce didn't wave when the Panama hat twisted around.

Trixie was raised high over the head of the boy.

Earl could make out the high-pitched yapping of the toy poodle. As Trixie struggled to jump out of Deuce's hands toward the window, the bus accelerated.

Standing in the middle of the street, Deuce watched the Greyhound move through the intersection and enter an on-ramp of a northbound freeway. He picked his way through honking cars to the curb and set Trixie down.

The poodle took off --- straight across the inter-section, dodging traffic. The last view Deuce had of the dog was as it scampered up the freeway ramp.

When he could safely do so, Deuce ran after the dog. Jogging up the ramp, the boy imagined the toy poodle chasing across lanes of the freeway traffic. A sixth sense told him he wouldn't be returning the small dog to its owner.

He was right.

When Deuce reached the top of the ramp, he saw a man walking along the edge of the freeway --- some 150 yards distant. He carried a red bag and wore a Panama hat, with Trixie under his arm.

Deuce raced to Earl and was greeted with a broad smile.

"How 'bout another card trick, son?"

"The pink lady came back!" exclaimed Deuce.

"I finally figured that out," nodded Earl, "by the dog." He brought Trixie higher to give her a kiss.

Upon their arrival back at the shoe store, Deuce spotted Maria sitting in back near the counter with an elderly man holding a cane. When the man turned his head, Deuce shouted out:

"Mr Weinstein!"

The storeowner was as impeccably dressed as ever. Dabbing at an eye with a handkerchief, he grinned as the joyful boy ran to him.

"Maria tells me," began Mr Weinstein, "that you've worked hard taking care of my store."

To prove how well he'd done, Deuce thought to turn over the money he'd received from sales. He wanted to ask Maria if the pink lady had returned with the Earl's money. Fidgeting, Deuce instead asked:

"Where'd you go?"

"To a hospital," explained the storeowner. "And the doctors would not release me until today."

"Are you okay?" asked Deuce.

"I am fine, but the doctors tell me I must stop working ... I must sell the store."

In the ensuing silence, the storeowner's gaze wandered over Earl the Whirl and the toy poodle which busied itself vainly searching for crumbs in the man's trouser cuffs.

"And who are you ... with the dog?"

The con man extended his hand. "T. Earl Stengal ... at your service."

"Stengal?" queried the storeowner. "Like the Yankee baseball manager?"

Earl truthfully nodded. "My uncle."

"Casey Stengal knew how to play the game," nodded Mr Weinstein.

And it's time for me to stop playing it, thought Earl.

Deuce touched the con man's arm and spoke to the storeowner. "He's been helping me with the customers."

The boy spoke again to Mr Weinstein. "I wish you could keep the store."

Mr Weinstein shook his head. "So do I, but what if I fainted with a customer?"

No one spoke for a long moment.

"I've enjoyed helping in your store," said Earl. "If I had the money, I'd---"

It occurred to the con man that he had less than $10 after purchasing his Greyhound ticket.

"You have this," said Deuce, holding up the ring with the red stone. "Use it for money."

Contemplating the ring, Earl took on a somber expression at the irony of the boy's offer. For once in my life, mused Earl, I gave something to someone ... and now ... it's coming back. He looked to Mr Weinstein and saw a tear floating from an eye. Trying to speak, Earl found his throat choked up. He coughed several times.

"I don't need a ring," insisted Deuce. He gave a troubled glance to Maria.

Earl the Whirl held up empty hands and started to say he had nothing to give in return for the ring. The silver-linked band of his watch stopped him.

He looked at the boy's empty wrists. "You need a watch, don't you?"

Deuce hesitated to speak..

Earl removed his timepiece. "This looks like a Rolex, but it's not a real one. I'd still like you to have it."

Man and boy solemnly exchanged ring and watch.

"Merry Christmas," said Deuce, as an afterthought.

The words unsettled the con man. It had been too many years since he'd heard those words ... with a gift. For a long moment, the two of them stood quietly before each other. In the boy's eyes, Earl could see a longing, a yearning which he himself also felt. Slowly ... the man opened his arms. Deuce moved forward, and they briefly embraced.

When they stepped back, the boy placed the watch on his wrist. Earl could not help but stare at his former timepiece.

"That's it!" he nearly shouted. *"The watch!"*

Earl looked around at startled faces, none of whom had any idea of what he spoke.

"It made me late for Tanya!" he tried to explain. "At noon today, I *forgot* to turn it back 21 minutes!"

Receiving blank stares, Earl decided not to attempt a further explanation. He turned to Mr Weinstein.

"Sir, this morning, the pawnbroker down the street offered $3,000 for this ring. Would you accept it as a downpayment on the purchase of your store?"

"Yes," said the storeowner, whose face took on a cynical grin. "But I know that pawnbroker. If he told you $3,000, it must be worth much more. I will give you an adjustment after we go to a honest jeweler for an appraisal."

As the two men shook hands on the deal, a taxi screeched to a stop before the store entrance.

Tanya emerged from the vehicle and ran into the store.

"You're here!" she cried out to Earl.

As Trixie happily pranced around the couple, Earl got his second embrace of the day.

When they came apart, Earl told her: "I'm buying this store for us ... and I don't need a loan."

"That's *wonderful!*" said Tanya. Some of the delight on her face faded.

"How many afternoons will you be working?" she inquired impishly.

Taken aback by the question, Earl was stumped. His answer would be real this time. He looked about, his eyes settling on Deuce.

"Son, will you be my partner in this store?"

Deuce nodded with enthusiasm. "Sure!"

Earl turned back to Tanya and told her: "One, maybe two."

When she released him from his third embrace, Tanya fished around in her purse and handed Earl the envelope of cash he'd given her earlier at the U.S. Grant.

"Your money," she told him.

Earl promptly handed it to Deuce.

The boy ran into the back room and returned with the *Les Miserables* book. Handing it to Mr Weinstein, Deuce told him:

"This is from shoe sales."

Opening the cover of the book and lifting out the cash, the storeowner merrily looked up. "Everyone receives a gift."

He handed the antique book back to Deuce. "This is yours ... along with my other books. You can leave them here until you have a place to keep them."

"Oh!" exclaimed Tanya. She hurried to the front of the store where she'd left her shopping bag. Bringing it back to Earl, she gave it to him.

He lifted out a rattan picnic box.

"For dinners on the beach," she explained...and received a kiss.

Tanya's eyes sparkled as she looked about the small group. Pointing to Maria, she said:

"Goodness, we've forgotten this lovely girl."

The attention of the others settled on Maria as she pulled from her small purse a piece of mistletoe and calmly spoke to everyone.

"I know what I want."

Tanya gayly smiled. "I think I know, too." The woman took the mistletoe and held it over the girl's head.

Maria flashed her dark eyes at Deuce.

The boy had been thinking of his new library and that *The Tenfold Return* truly worked.

Blushing, Deuce stepped over to Maria.

"Merry Christmas," he whispered before lightly touching his lips to hers.

It was a beginning.

❄❄❄

For Loved Ones, Friends, and Others who return books slowly, additional copies of this book can be purchased from:

>Pacific Rim Press
>Playa del Pacifica
>Post Office Box 220
>Carlsbad, CA 92018

Please enclose $14.95, plus $1.20 tax (if res. Calif,). We'll pay the shipping. Be sure to specify how you wish your book *autographed,.*

Autographed editions of Robert Lawrence Holt's other books are also available from Pacific Rim Press. They include:

Good Friday (hardbound)	$14.95
Sweetwater (hardbound)	14.95
Peacemaker (hardbound)	17.95
Peacemaker (trade paperback)	14.95
Bonds (softbound)	7.95
Straight Teeth (softbound)	8.95

(please include tax if Calif resident)